I0576447

LIVING SPRINGS PUBLISHERS PRESENTS:

STORIES THROUGH THE AGES BABY BOOMERS PLUS 2020

Compiled and edited by:
Henry E. Peavler, Dan Peavler, and Jacqueline Veryle Peavler

Introduction by: Henry Peavler and Dan Peavler

Short Stories by: Charles Warren, Jim Gish, Anne Hill, Chuck Jackson, Richard Key, Barbara Mujica, David Parish, Kaye George, Jim Tritten, Don Carter, Patricia Lee, Brad Bennett, Elizabeth Bobst, Sandra Brooks, Wayne Fowler, Eric Rosenbaum, and David Tarpenning

Each story in this collection is a work created from the imagination or experience of the author. The views expressed in the stories do not necessarily reflect the views of Living Spring Publishers L.L.P.

Copyright 2020

by Living Springs Publishers LLP

Paperback ISBN: 978-1-7344593-5-7

eBook ISBN: 978-1-7344593-6-4

Library of Congress Control Number: 2020944448

Living Springs Publishers

www.LivingSpringsPublishers.com

Cover design by Jacqueline Peavler

When an eagle appears, it signals a new beginning and provides the stamina and resilience to endure difficulties - it bestows freedom and the courage to look ahead.

We dedicate this book to the eagle and all it symbolizes.

Contents

Synopses

A Wing and A Prayer: Charles Warren has won first prize in the 2020 Baby Boomers Plus contest. He shares a marvelous tale of a young British boy's experience with American pilots during World War II. The chance interaction between the two has consequences far beyond the end of the war, lasting a lifetime. Well crafted, told without rancor or blame.

Into the Stormtroopers: This is a must-read story about the tumultuous events that abruptly thrust Don Carter into the international spotlight and an adventure of a lifetime. When a long-forgotten college photography assignment is suddenly linked to a presidential assassination attempt, the Secret Service, FBI and US Assistant District Attorney abruptly show up at the author's door. Don't miss this gripping, page-turning mystery about events that every baby-boomer will remember. Don won second prize with his story.

A Silent Victory: In Second Century AD Roman Scotland, Corellia, an abused slave girl, is determined to save a young Roman legionary who she finds near death on the battlefield adjacent to her village. She will need all her strength and intelligence to outwit her cruel slave owners and tend secretly to this young man. Patricia Lee wins third place with her suspenseful story that explores how human persistence and endurance are qualities slavery and disgrace cannot extinguish.

Attack of the Communist Hordes: Brad Bennett shares a marvelous true story of events on an airbase as a result of the assassination of President John Kennedy. One of those stories that could be funny if it weren't so incredibly fouled up. It makes you wonder what the people in charge are thinking. Be sure to read this one.

Your Mother's Sock: A poignant story of parents in an assisted living facility. That sentence probably conveys emotions enough but Elizabeth Bobst's well written account of the heartbreak, angst, tension and even humor of the situation must be experienced. Don't miss reading this marvelous story.

Silent Tears: It was 1966 and America was going through unprecedented changes. A young girl lands a coveted job with a local politician only to discover a horrible secret. She is the only one who knows. What should she do? What would you do? Sandra Brooks has crafted a magnificent story that leaves the reader with an uncomfortable guilty conscience as though we are all complicit in the cover-up. This is excellent reading.

Fun, Fun, Fun with Dick and Jane: A playful story about a precocious pair of students and the havoc they wreak on a helpless pre-school teacher trying to impart knowledge using, possibly, an old McGuffey Reader. The repetition of words drives poor Ohmie to distraction and the teacher to the telephone to call Ohmie's mother to come and get him. An entertaining tale from the pen, pen, pen of Wayne Fowler.

Fins Fatal Flop: Kaye George's characters are so well crafted you can feel the tension in crisis and share the emotion in tragedy. This story takes place in a strip-tease bar but there is nothing shabby about the people who care for each other and do whatever it takes to protect themselves from the bad guys. Great entertainment, good reading.

Deluxe Accom: Author Jim Gish's tale of a college party gone terribly wrong rings true for those coming of age in the 60's and 70's. What started as a normal get together for liberated boys and girls, ended in tragedy for everyone involved. This story is hard-hitting, realistic and well written.

A Day with 3D: New Zealand, in 1970, had a very romantic appeal to our young heroine, coveting the opportunity of a job in a far-away land. Leaving the safety of her native Florida with a new teaching degree and a job in the teacher starved unknown over 8,000 miles away, author Anne Hill has created a compelling adventure that is both poignant and gratifying.

Welcome to Vietnam: Chuck Jackson shares his incredible story of life as a Special Forces member of an Air Force Pararescue Team, Da Nang, 1968. Another of those stories that should never be lost to the caprices of time. These men and women deserve to be remembered for the champions that they were and are.

Thanks Mussolini: Richard Key has shared a memoir of a family trip to Italy in 1996. The story reminds us what travel in a foreign country could be like in the old days, before the internet and cell phones. We follow the author's family to Bari, the city where his wife was born, and relive the train ride where things go south as the family heads north to Venice.

Ahmed the Tailor: An extremely well fashioned story of the unlikely relationship of an Iraqi tailor and a young Marine Lieutenant. With enduring patience our hero bridges the gap between two cultures and creates a small victory in a very human, personal way. Excellent writing by author Barbara Mujica.

Breakfast Crisis: A heart-wrenching story of a teenager's rapidly deteriorating relationship with his father. David Parish's tale of a father's betrayal and his son's attempt to understand and come to grips with the emotional fallout is a must read for everyone who enjoys a well written account of the anguish of growing up.

The Ping-Pong War: If you doubt that a sports contest in a United Nations International School in New York, doesn't have far-reaching implications, think again. Eric Rosenbaum shares a fantastic account of negotiating the halls of a school where none of the students speak like you, look like you or come from the same place as you. A spectacular story, well written and timely. Thank you Eric.

Smoke from Indian Fires: David Tarpenning has gifted us a marvelous story about idyllic life on the farm when the only hint of war was in far off lands, overseas; no threat to us. Life wasn't always easy, but one could live it as seen fit. Then December 7, 1941 that life ended forever. This is a well-crafted story that should be read in every classroom in America.

The Illustrated Man: Appearances aren't always what they seem to be. This story takes place on an airplane but could happen anywhere. A situation seen as a dire threat to our very existence turns out to be something entirely different. Jim Tritten's tale of one such threat misinterpretation makes for excellent reading.

Introduction

"Every great dream begins with a dreamer. Always remember you have within you the strength, the patience, and the passion to reach for the stars and change the world."
Harriet Tubman.

Living Springs Publishers is extremely happy to share these varied and entertaining stories from authors around the world, who had the imagination and talent to create seventeen short stories which make up "Stories Through the Ages Baby Boomers Plus 2020". As in previous contests, we received entries from across the United States, but, somewhat different in the 2020 book, many worldwide authors submitted stories, giving this year's book an international flavor.

This year's winning authors remind us of the past, weaving tales of agony, hardship, happiness, and hope. We thank them for having the courage and confidence to submit their stories. Creativity and writing talent are subjective and difficult to judge. Opinions as to what constitutes a 'great' story vary from reader to reader and, although our judges disagreed often, we feel the final choices make for an entertaining and powerful book.

Students of history, young and old, will find real treasure in the pages of this book. People, of a certain age, will relive important memories of the past through the eyes of those who were directly involved. Our 2020 book includes different, illuminating stories of young people carrying a weight too heavy for youth during the time of war. From crossing paths with a would-be assassin, to unforeseen consequences of the assassination of President Kennedy, to enduring the Vietnam conflict, or listening to confessions in a strip joint; the unique imagination and creativity of the authors give us different perspectives of the beautiful, and sometimes troubling world we all share.

The poignant and entertaining manner in which the authors crafted their stories allow the reader to escape into a world of mystery with human persistence and endurance. The stories from the past give us a prism to look thorough, allowing everyone to imagine a better future. Creating hope in a better world, where dreams can become a reality.

A Wing and a Prayer
By Charles Warren

The years have nearly healed the wingspan-wide scar in the wood. The tumult of brambles and bushes that first covered the sheared stumps and scorched ground were replaced by pert saplings and now, half a century later, those young conifers are twice the height of a man.

I'll be gone by the time they catch up with the rest of the trees around them but, for as long as my health will let me, I'll keep coming back every year with my roses. Never once have I wanted to stop. Never once has walking up the long farm track to the wood felt like a ritual. Much of that grey winter day in 1944 is as clear to me now as it has ever been. As I grow older, its pull seems to gather strength and this time, as I kneel to lay my flowers on a coppery bed of fallen pine needles, a tear clings to my cheek in the November wind.

When I straighten my back and turn to make my way down the long shallow slope of the track, I can see a figure moving up the hill towards me.

***

I walked across my father's empty meadow to a low

hedge of hawthorn and dog rose and watched the Americans loading bombs into the bellies of their silver Fortresses. I wanted to fly -- I'd be old enough in a couple of years – not in a bomber like these, but in a fighter. Father said the war would be over soon and farmers were needed on the land, not in the air. What's more, he wasn't going to let the Germans take another child of his.

'Hey, Kid.' It was Dan, one of the airmen. A lot of them came down here to smoke. A quiet spot. Some of them talked to me. Others wanted to be alone, pulling on their Lucky Strikes and staring somewhere only they could see. Sometimes they brought their letters down here to read, away from their comrades. Once I'd heard a man sobbing and another time I'd turned back home with a surge of embarrassment when I started to overhear an airman talking aloud to his mother as if she was standing next to him in the field.

Dan was always friendly. He said I reminded him of his 'kid brother'.

'You flying tomorrow?' I asked him.

'Maybe.' Dan stretched over the hedge and gave me a slab of chocolate. He tipped his head back to stare up at the grey skies. 'Weather's bad, I guess they might call it off.'

I passed back a box of eggs, still warm from where I had removed them from beneath a pair of affronted hens.

'Where are you going?'

'You know I can't tell you that, David.' Dan grinned. 'You might be a Kraut spy.'

I laughed, a little too loudly. My parents distrusted the well-fed American fliers with their informality and clean-cut uniforms. So, I, like many of the other teenagers in the village, adored them. I liked to think it was more than that too, more than their bright vigour in an England bleached grey by war. I spoke to some of them, so I thought I knew their secrets, that they wept for home and sometimes they were afraid.

'Dan?' I knew Dan best of all. He was a navigator in the Missy May, where he sat alone in a tiny compartment below the two pilots.

'Yes, Kid.' I could not have been more than three years younger than Dan but I rather liked being called Kid. I thought it was a sign of friendship and it was a lot nicer than being called 'boy' by so many of my father's friends.

'I thought you were going home soon, back to...'

'Idaho. Yeah, so did I.' He tossed the cigarette away to land with scores of others scattered among the tufts of wet grass. 'Thought I'd get to see Mom and Dad and my stupid brother for Christmas. But they've extended the tour, 30 instead of 25 now.'

He looked straight at me. 'Thirty missions and each

time a few ships don't come back... those are lousy odds, Kid.'

***

The low drone of the first returning aircraft reached me as I swept the floor of my father's barn, a fine cloud of hammered dirt and corn dust rolling behind each push of the broom. I stood the broom by the wall and ran into the drizzle, scattering a mob of house sparrows as I crossed the muddy yard to a cart track and began trotting up a shallow rise to a stand of pine trees. The view was much better there than down by the hedge.

Huddled together just outside the base's perimeter, the trees had survived when a tent city of labourers from the other side of the Atlantic had arrived with their spluttering bulldozers to level the field and lay down a triangle of concrete runways and tear-drop hardstands where the glinting Fortresses stood between flights.

Out of breath, I arrived in time to see the first bomber square up the woods, lighter without its bombs and fuel and twitching in the crosswinds. Sometimes there would be a straggler, minutes behind all the rest, with one of its four engines burnt out or a wing ragged with splinter damage, but this aircraft was untouched, the co-pilot giving me a brief wave as it ruffled the conifers and skimmed down on to the runway. More were dropping from the clouds, waiting their turn to land. From the wood I could see the ground crews and senior officers crowded on and around the base's little red brick control tower, counting each aircraft home.

Two more Fortresses roared over my head before I saw Missy May. I knew her number, yellow four-foot-high characters on her tail, and there was Missy May herself, a boyish fantasy painted on the aircraft's nose, winking at me as she whisked by. I waved and turned to go, but stopped when the next Fortress staggered into line, one engine trailing a pencil line of smoke, another black and still. I caught the smell of burnt oil and rubber as its blackened underside filled the sky above me, no sign of its landing wheels. The aircraft tilted and sank beyond the pines and I heard the bells of the fire trucks and ambulances as it screamed down the runway on its belly, trailing sparks and broken metal. In my mind's eye I saw the ten terrified boys pinned inside the tortured aircraft. I tried to mutter the prayer I used to say every morning at school, but my words were snatched away in the thunder of the next aircraft.

***

'Mum says I can't give you any more eggs. She says the hens have gone off laying. Dad says it's all the noise your planes make. I think it's just the time of year.'

'It don't matter.' Dan's hand shook a little as he passed

a box of cigarettes over the hedge. 'For your mom.' He didn't look at me this time but watched the ground crews working on the nearest Fortress in the last of the evening light.

'The guys that belly landed, they all made it.'

'I saw them come in. I was worried...' I trailed off. Whatever I said sounded inadequate. How much could I really know about what it took to ride in the freezing air at 20,000 ft as black balls of flak shook my trembling aircraft and flung shreds of brute steel through its aluminum hide? Or to see 27 tons of aircraft and ten men turned into smoke and spinning debris by a direct hit.

Dan was silent for a few seconds before he spoke again, his face suddenly lineless, like a mannequin's. 'We lost three more ships today.'

'I'm sorry.' I didn't know what else to say. Until now, Dan had confined his conversation to basic stuff that I asked him about the aircraft, to his family, - 'You really do remind me of my kid brother' - and ribbing me - 'You're both kinda dumb'.

'One of the guys, he'd been here with me since '42. Left his watch behind.'

'His watch?'

'He thought it was his lucky charm. Turns out, he was right.'

David knew he shouldn't ask, but the question sprang out of him all the same. 'What's yours?'

'We all have them. You know, an old letter, a Bible, a girlfriend's picture…. What's mine? You are, Kid.'

'Me?'

'So stick around. Keep looking out for me. Just four more missions… will you do that?'

Again, I fumbled for the right words so, at once thrilled and frightened, I said: 'Yes, yes, I will. I should get back; I'm supposed to be stacking bales.'

'Bales?'

'Straw bales. They're heavy. I have to do a lot more now all the hands have joined up.'

'No brother to help?'

'I had a sister. She was nursing in London. She got killed when they bombed her hospital.' When I tried to picture her, I could only see that starchy photograph of her in uniform in our front room.

'I'm sorry, David.' Dan looked carefully into my face. 'This will all be over soon.'

He walked slowly back up the slope to the runway and the silhouettes of the resting aircraft.

I was splitting logs the next morning when I heard the first engines cough and splutter. The smell of gasoline fumes and oil drifted into the farmyard as scores more shuddered into life and the laden Fortresses began to haul themselves up into the half-light. I knew this was a dangerous time as bombers from stations all over the county groped through the cloud and dark to gather in formations that stretched for miles. I picked up another lump of long-dead oak, stood it up and swung the axe, the two halves clattering away from one another.

I thought about my promise to Dan, but what could I do? I couldn't even tell one dark aircraft from another as they clambered into the sky. So, I pictured Dan in his flying gear at his tiny seat at the feet of the pilot and, watched by one of the farm's black and white cats, said a prayer for him. This time I got to the end of it.

When I bent to pick up another log, I noticed my mother standing in the shed doorway. I wondered if she had seen me stop working to pray and blushed.

'Your breakfast's ready, dear.'

I stood the axe against a wall and joined her outside where the dawn was filling the yard with colour and the hum of the aircraft was beginning to fade.

'Is Dan flying today?'

'I think so, mum.'

'That's a lot he's asked of you.' He had told her of his promise, begging her not to tell his father.

'They're the ones in danger. We're all right down here.'

'I know.'

'Maybe one day I'll go see him in America. When the war's over.'

'If your father can spare you.'

'Maybe I'll meet that brother of his.'

She placed a hand on my shoulder and together we turned toward the farmhouse.

***

I rinsed the old blackened roasting tin. My mother tore up a stale white loaf and dropped the pieces in the tin. She always liked to join me for this job and already the farm's squadron of black and white cats and kittens had begun to circle at our feet. I put the tin on the barn floor and poured milk from a steel churn over the bread. Ten glossy hummocks of fur assembled round the tin. I'd wanted one as a pet, but my father said they had a job to do, catching the rats, mice and sparrows and anything else that nibbled or pecked our stores of feed, seed and harvested grain.

My mother and I watched the cats jostling and listened to the patter of their feeding.

My father joined us, silent for a seconds before he spoke. 'David. I need your help up at the Long Meadows.'

'Now?'

'No time like the present.' It was one of his stock phrases, as worn out as he seemed to me, with his thinning hair, his long back starting to stoop beneath decades of toil... and loss.

'But...'

'You'll need your boots. It's muddy up there.'

'I need to wait here, for the – '

'You need to earn your keep. You and your bloody Americans. They've got a job to do and so have we.'

When he pulled off his cap and scratched his sparse hair, I knew he was irritated. I also knew he wouldn't rage or shout. He's not raised his voice to anyone since that letter came in 1940 to say his daughter wasn't coming home. So, I always did what he asked. At least I could do that for my parents.

'I'll get my boots and coat.'

I heard my mother's tiny sigh and caught her eye. She smiled faintly. 'I'll have the tea on for when you get back,' she said.

My father replaced his cap and nodded. 'We shouldn't be too long.'

***

I watched the skies and listened. I thought we would have finished by now. Instead I was still two miles from home, helping father move cattle from one meadow to another, funneling the animals through a gateway. Lowing and puffing, misting the air with their meaty breath, they had churned the ground around the gate to a pond of knee-deep mud. Now and then one would panic and spurt away from the rest. It was my job to wave my arms, whistle and turn these strays back into the melee at the gate. My father was ahead of me, cajoling the cattle through the mud.

When I next looked up, I saw the first of the returning bombers swim out of the clouds. I might get back to see at least a few of them land. Maybe that would be enough. Maybe that would count.

Father was pushing the gate shut behind the last animal. 'All done,' he said. He glanced up and then at me. 'We could have got this done a lot quicker if you had kept your mind on the job.'

He circled the pool of mud and joined me. We both watched as a single Fortress sagged lower than the rest, bleeding smoke from a wing, the rest of the flight keeping high, giving way to the faltering aircraft. It lurched through a set of shallow bounds in the low sky as the pilot fought for height. After the last, it dropped from sight.

A ball of tangerine flame flared on the horizon. I jumped as if I had been kicked when I heard the thump of the explosion. Smoke as black as coal began to stack in the windless air over the spot where I had seen the flame.

'That was in the pines over the farm.' His father's voice was drained of its usual rigour. 'We'd better go home.'

***

I remember that two mile drive. We sat in silence. My father knew what I was thinking. All the way home he stole glances at me. I was praying, rolling the words over and over in my head: 'Please don't let it be Dan, please don't let it be the Missy May.'

It was, of course. I hadn't been there, counting them home.

I don't remember a great deal about the rest of that day, just my father's face as he held my arms and tried to reason with me and my mother's embrace.

They wouldn't let me near the wood but two days later I stole away and found what was left of the Missy May, an empty carcass lying flat among the sheared trees and picked clean by a salvage team from the base. The nose of the aircraft looked as if it had been punched with a giant fist before what was left of the fuel exploded, smearing its silver flanks with soot. Of Dan and his comrades there was no sign.

As for Missy May, her impossible curves were scratched and scarred. Her eye caught mine and I saw mockery in her leering wink, so I turned away from the aircraft and walked slowly home.

After that, I stayed away from the airfield – I was bad luck - though I still watched them come and go and in June

1945 I was there when the village turned out to see them off on their long flights back to America and the airfield was suddenly silent and empty.

***

I straighten my back and start back down the track. A few hundred yards away, the approaching man's coat is a shot of royal blue against the browns of the dead leaves in the hedges and the ploughed field next to him.

Other than these annual visits I have little to do with this place anymore. I left the farm as soon as I could and my disappointed father gave up the tenancy when he retired. Beyond the trees, a go-cart club plays about on the old runways. Ivy, brambles and neglect have subdued the huts where Dan and his comrades ate, slept and smoked and that little control tower was pulled down ten years ago.

I offer a brief smile to the stranger who has stopped as if to wait for me. He is about my age.

'Excuse me, sir.' The accent is American, the inflection dimly familiar. 'I'm looking for a wood where a plane crashed in the last war – a Flying Fortress. A guy at the airfield said he thought it was up here.'

'It's that low stretch of the wood, there.' I point up the hill and when he turns away from me to look, I study his face. I speak to fill up the moment. 'I've just been there myself. Every year, the day of the crash.'

'I've never made it until now. Life slips by you but fifty years on it suddenly seems important. My older brother was in that plane.'

'Dan?'

'Yes, he was called Dan...'

'I knew him. I grew up here, in the war, on this farm. We used to talk. He spoke of you... of his younger brother.'

The American is silent for a moment before he extends his hand. 'It's David, isn't it? He wrote about you. I read all his letters again before I came over.'

I draw a long hard breath and for a few seconds each of sees 21-year-old Dan as if he is standing on the track between us.

'I was supposed to watch out for him,' I blurt. 'Only, I wasn't there the day he crashed...'

'He said something about it in his letters, how he knew you waited for him and the other guys. Back then, I thought it was kinda nice for him. Now I'm not sure he should have asked you...it was quite a weight for a kid of 17.'

'A lot of very young people carried a lot of weight in those days.'

'I guess.' The American turns his gaze back from the wood to me and smiles softly. 'I know about the crash. They died on account of getting shot up, they lost two engines and the Missy May wouldn't fly true anymore. Nothing else.

They'd have been in the same trouble, whether you were there or not.'

'I've told myself that many times, but...'

'Well, I'm his brother. Listen to me, if not to yourself.'

Again we fall into silence until Dan's brother seems to come to a decision. 'Would you wait for me, David? After I have been here, I'm going to the church in the village. There's a little memorial there apparently.'

'I know it.'

'I'm going to take a look and say a prayer. For Dan.'

'I've not prayed for anything very much for a long time.' I realise it sounds rather brutal.

'Well, you can keep me company,' he says quietly and looks away from me, back at the wood, at the slump in the line of trees.

Finally, I find my voice. 'I would like that.'

He nods and smiles again.

I watch Dan's brother walk steadily towards the pines before turning my back on them and returning down the hill to wait.   end

Charles Warren

 Charles has been a UK national newspaper journalist for more than 25 years. He lives in Surrey, southern England, with his wife, two grown-up children and a very small cat. His stories have been published in print in the UK by the Earlyworks Press, Writers' Forum magazine, Scribble magazine and on competition websites. He's a big admirer of American fiction, especially writers such as William Gay, Charles Frazier, Kent Haruf, Daniel Woodrell and James Lee Burke. At the end of last year he secured his first US publication when his historical crime story was printed by the Tulip Tree Review literary magazine in Colorado. He is thrilled to make another US appearance with Living Springs Publishers.

Into the Stormtroopers
By Don Carter

"It was a bright cold day in April, and the clocks were striking thirteen." George Orwell, 1984

As a younger man I seldom gave thought to motivation or consequence. I felt compelled to take risks – to seek out the dark places and walk with the beasts – but the nearest I got to reflection was when I inevitably picked myself up, checked for injuries and wondered, "What the hell was I thinking?"

As an older man I've struggled with the emotional fallout that comes from second-guessing one's actions but despite some feelings of regret, I believe my *raison d'être* was well intentioned. I like to think I climbed under the bed in the middle of the night, faced the monsters and dragged them into the light so that we might all better understand the hatefulness that grows in the shadows we choose to ignore.

When I was a freshman at the School of the Art Institute of Chicago, I set out to expose these darker places. Little did I suspect that the images I captured would one day attract international attention and the FBI, subpoena in hand, would come looking for the monsters I uncovered.

More on that later.

*****

Part One – Of White Power and White Guilt
November 1974

It was one of *those* November days in Chicago. The savage wind and rain – whipped into a predatory frenzy by the whitecaps on Lake Michigan – stalked victims up and down Michigan Avenue. It was a dismal, atheist rain, just one degree short of converting to sleet.

It was a perfect day for hunting Nazis.

I turned my back against the rain and prayed my knit cap and raised collar would help sell my disguise. The term *skinhead* hadn't yet come into vogue, but I was fairly certain a *longhair* would not be welcome inside Nazi Party headquarters. I was trying to look like a rough and tumble longshoreman but suspected I looked more like Mike Nesmith of the Monkees.

The target of my photo-documentary was an organization calling itself the National Socialist Party of America (NSPA), which rumor held was headquartered in the Marquette Park neighborhood on the city's far south side. White supremacist Frank Collin formed the NSPA in 1966 after being dismissed from the National Socialist White People's Party (NSWPP) which had evolved from the original American Nazi Party founded by George Lincoln Rockwell. In a few years Collin would become the subject of extensive media coverage when he announced the NSPA, dressed in full Nazi Stormtrooper regalia, intended to march through Skokie, Illinois, home to a vast enclave of Holocaust survivors.

The streets of Marquette Park were deserted when I arrived. Its shoe cobblers, TV repairmen and fortunetellers had closed their doors against the repugnant weather and its residents had taken refuge behind thick, faded curtains The aging, old-world population seemed reluctant to give up its secret but when I found myself staring gape-mouthed at George Lincoln Rockwell Hall I realized the NSPA was not the clandestine operation I had expected.

Rockwell Hall had the unmistakable look of a Nazi Party headquarters. The two-story brick fortress was built with steel reinforced doors, barricaded windows, and a swastika banner flying high above the pediment. But the real giveaway, the images that jolted me like a jackboot to the solar plexus, were the brazen racist messages broadcast across the second story walls.

I stood frozen before the reinforced door, my inertia finally broken when a group of goose-stepping Nazis marched up the street and a fresh regiment of goose pimples marched down my spine. The placards they carried spewed loathsome messages and their shirts bore the stark, unmistakable likeness of a swastika encircled by the words "WHITE POWER".

There's a scene in The Wizard of Oz in which the Scarecrow, Tin Man and Cowardly Lion slip into the Wicked Witch's castle by following the Winkie Guards through an imposing gate. As they fall in line behind the last guard the Cowardly Lion vainly attempts to conceal his tail inside his coat. Like some absurd Winkie parody the Nazis marched past me and entered single file into their fortress. I confirmed that my own tail (that is to say my ponytail) was safely hidden inside my coat and then I fell in line behind the last Nazi and slipped into the claustrophobic confines of Rockwell Hall.

When the disconcerting thud of a dead bolt sounded behind me the stale air seemed to compress like the muffled atmosphere inside a decompressing airplane. With my head down to avoid eye contact I ricocheted off brusque neo-Nazis who seemed oblivious to my presence. It hadn't occurred to me that they might think of me as just another bored, hate-mongering teenager and for the time being my mission remained hidden.

The room was dark and the musky air felt tainted with radioactive levels of testosterone. I wandered past drab walls punctuated with racist posters and feigned interest in dilapidated racks spilling over with xenophobic propaganda. On the farthest wall there hung an illuminated Nazi Party flag. In the monochromatic gloom its brilliant red and white hues shown like the glowing embers from a thousand burning books.

NSPA leader Frank Collin was middle-aged, diminutive and balding. He could have been the neighborhood butcher or insurance agent if not for the swastika on his arm and the pistol on his hip. Collin was rallying his troops for a propaganda blitzkrieg when I approached and revealed the camera hidden beneath my coat. He slowly sized me up as the voices in the room took on the guttural resonance of a pride of mountain lions eyeing their prey and doing the math. In Collin's unreadable eyes I felt the monster's invisible arms slither around my chest and send my lungs chasing air.

Frank Collin was many things including a candidate for the local alderman's seat. His unambiguous campaign slogan – WHITE MAN FIGHT – was plastered on the side of Rockwell Hall four decades before populist politicians would develop coded language to relay the same message. I recovered my breath and reminded Collin of a politician's need for exposure – a pitch that made my stomach lurch as the stark propaganda films of Leni Riefenstahl sprang to

mind. He broke from his deliberation and summoned his men to pose before the flag for a quick group shot – just like one big happy Aryan family.

After Collin's troops dispersed, I took a seat next to a quiet man wearing a brown shirt and a black gun. The young Nazi had the abbreviated syntax of a man uncomfortable talking to others but when I asked about his pistol he brightened and unholstered the weapon. He emptied the bullets from their chambers and lined them up on the desk before me. "See how the tips are hollowed out?" he asked. "They're called 'dum-dum bullets'. They expand on impact to inflict maximum damage."

The term was new to me. In a few years dum-dum bullets would enter the national vocabulary (and the national debate on gun control) when a gunman would fire a similar bullet into the President of the United States.

I guiltily continued my charade as an enthusiastic pupil and gradually pried open the door into the young man's guarded isolation. As he coddled the powerful weapon in his hands a subdued self-satisfaction began to lubricate his speech.

"Dum-dum bullets make a small hole when they go in, but a BIG hole when they come out."

His disarming demeanor was the antithesis of his unsettling words. Here sat a soft-spoken young man, marginally older than me, a man who came of age during the summer of love, flower power and the peace movement, and yet some unknown circumstance had led him down this dark, hateful path. He calmly spoke about killing with the emotional velocity typically reserved for ordering lunch. I imagined this carnal exchange, cold steel on warm flesh, would somehow deliver the psychological carbohydrates needed to feed his inner demons and sustain him through another day.

As the other Nazis returned to Rockwell Hall, I again felt the feral air compact around me. I longed to escape into

the frigid Chicago dusk, but I hadn't produced "the shot" –
the one image that captured the essence of my experience.
In other words, I had yet to drag the monster out from
under the bed and into the light.

My subject had relaxed in his role as weapons expert so
I positioned him before a portrait of Adolf Hitler. In the
moment he raised his gun I came face to face with the lethal
hollow tips nestled inside each chamber.

Click.

The monster was captured on a 35-millimeter prison of
film.

*****

My mind has replayed the hours spent inside NSPA
headquarters many times over and while the conversations
have faded from exact recall, I still remember the hollow
feeling of remorse that followed me home that day. It
wasn't Frank Collin or the young neo-Nazi with the bullet
fetish that upset me. It was my own clandestine façade, my
own revolver of guilt that fired the hollow-tipped bullets of
shame into my psyche.

I let a group of white supremacists believe that I was
one of them because the urge to do otherwise was
suppressed by a well-developed survival instinct. George
Orwell once cautioned, "He wears a mask and his face
grows to fit it". I didn't think I was in danger of succumbing

to an outbreak of racism or catching some neo-fascist infection. All of my liberal inoculations were up to date. No, the sepsis crawling beneath my skin was more like the associative guilt that Michael Herr described in his Vietnam memoir *Dispatches*; "I went there behind the crude but serious belief that you had to be able to look at anything, serious because I acted on it and went, crude because I didn't know, it took the war to teach it, that you were as responsible for everything you saw as you were for everything you did."

Time spent in the company of white supremacists infects the soul with white guilt; a cultural remorse derived from membership in a race that has for centuries, slaughtered, enslaved and banned people of color. The catalyst of the guilt gnawing at my consciousness was the memory of how I so eagerly and easily sold my disguise. It was the liability of this deception that quietly chafed at my moral sensibilities for years and it was the unresolved culpability of omission that eventually metastasized into a malignant lump of regret.

I had no idea how far my photo documentary would travel when I walked out of George Lincoln Rockwell Hall, but in hindsight there was a great deal I didn't know that day. I didn't know that Frank Collin would win a frightening 16% of the primary vote in his bid for public office or that these same Chicago Nazis would gain international notoriety when the Supreme Court would allow them to demonstrate in Skokie, Illinois. I didn't know that Collin would eventually be ousted from power when he was exposed as the son of Jewish immigrants or that he would go to prison for molesting young boys inside Nazi Party headquarters.

And I most certainly didn't know that the FBI, armed with a subpoena, would visit my office in search of the monsters I held captive on a tiny strip of film. It wasn't Frank Collin they were seeking. They were looking for the quiet young Nazi with an unhealthy infatuation with guns; a man who possessed an even stronger infatuation with a young actress named Jodie Foster. The FBI was chasing the murky past of John W. Hinckley Jr., the disturbed gunman who shot down President Ronald Reagan and three others on a Washington D.C. sidewalk.

*****

Part Two – The De-Evolution of Truth
May 1981

The phone rang at dawn and as I pulled the receiver close a metallic shout from the other end jolted me upright and awake.

"FEDS SEIZE NAZI PIX!"

"Wha ...?"

"The New York Post. Front page. FEDS ... SEIZE ... NAZI ... PIX!"

Five minutes later I stood sockless at the corner newsstand, scrutinizing the front page of the New York Post. Two familiar Nazis stared back. Adolf Hitler's portrait hung in the background, his stare intense and chilling. A young neo-Nazi with a raised pistol in hand stood in the foreground – his expression unreadable and lifeless – but no less chilling. My eyes went to the photo credit beneath the picture where I found my name.

I was no journalist. When I took the picture I was a teenage art student shooting an exposé of Nazi activity for a college photography assignment. If I'd been a journalist, I would have written down the names of my subjects. Instead I'd spent the past two months struggling to learn the true identity of the man now staring back at me from the newsstand.

I secured the resources of the *New York Post* to help uncover the truth but when the District Attorney in Washington D.C. got wind of my "bombshell" photo-documentary the truth proved irrelevant. No longer interested in the young Nazi's true identity, *The Post* ran the story on page one because, "Yesterday, in a surprise move, two [FBI] agents quietly returned to the Manhattan office of photographer Don Carter with a subpoena for the negatives."[1]

Today the word truth is conveniently presented between a pair of bobbing fingers. Tabloid television, fake news, and alternative facts contribute to a systemic American malady symptomized by "quotation truth". Much like "Newspeak", the language George Orwell created in his novel *1984*, the corrosive de-evolution of truth radiating from Washington and perpetuated by mercenary media outlets is designed to create an alternate reality – a reality that rewrites history and contradicts all that we know to be true. Orwell forewarned, "The very concept of objective truth is fading out of the world. Lies will pass into history."

Do we give up all hope of objective truth the moment we let others manipulate our perception of reality? Once we take that leap of faith – whether with a parent, teacher, political party or the press – do we become nothing more than the manipulated sycophants of a thousand well-orchestrated lies?

In 1981 it hadn't occurred to me that truth could be subjective, opinion, or mutable and my single-minded mission had been to discover the truth (sans-quotation marks) about the pictures that would soon make their way into magazines around the world. The September 1981 issue of *American Photographer* magazine reported,

> While agencies like Sygma and Gamma/Liaison were turning over their files for pictures of young blond Nazis, Carter was painstakingly trying to identify the young man who had posed for him before a picture of Adolf Hitler. Eager to obtain a positive i.d., Carter, now a videotape editor in New York City, called the Post and offered exclusive first rights if the paper would do the legwork.[2]

At a midnight meeting in lower Manhattan with *New York Post* columnist Steve Dunleavy (the tabloid TV reporter better known for his work on *A Current Affair*) the newspaper agreed to turn the images over to their contacts at the Secret Service. The subsequent article revealed that, "Two days later a Secret Service Agent told The Post he was "90% sure" of the man's identity."

After two months of fruitless research, the FBI

subpoena had come as a welcome development, a signal that perhaps the truth would finally be revealed. Could the young neo-Nazi be, as the Justice Department suspected, the same man who had recently attempted to assassinate President Ronald Reagan? Was it possible I'd spent an afternoon discussing hollow-tipped bullets with the insane gunman John Hinckley Jr.?

*****

Two Months Earlier

It was a bright cold day in April when I heard the news that Hinckley had gunned down President Reagan, Secret Service agent Tim McCarthy, police officer Thomas Delahanty and White House Press Secretary James Brady, who succumbed to his wounds decades later. In the days following the shooting, sketchy details of Hinckley's involvement in the American Nazi Party surfaced. Like a ghost rattling its chains outside memory's doorway, something in these reports was haunting me. For days I consciously ignored what my subconscious would not and when the weekend arrived, I succumbed to an irrepressible urge to catch up on events with the Sunday *New York Times*.

> 25-year-old John Hinckley is charged with attempting to assassinate President Reagan, and his apparent fascination with the National Socialist Party and his brief reported association with the

neo-Nazi group remain an important focus of the Federal Government's investigation.[3]

In the years between shooting my photo documentary and the shooting of the president, Frank Collin had lost control of the National Socialist Party of America and a new generation of leaders had emerged. *The Times* article reported,

> Two successive leaders of the American Nazi group, Mr. Allen and Harold Covington, have said that Mr. Hinckley was a member ... Mr. Allen, the party leader, said that "character assessment" reports from Mr. Breda to Mr. Collin, the party leader at the time of the Skokie march, suggested that "basically, he was uncontrollable" and openly preached violence.[3]

The National Socialist Party? Mr. Collin? The Skokie march? It took about a thousand gigawatts of clues but the cerebral light bulb finally switched on and for the first time since the shooting I took a good look at the images of John Hinckley Jr. in the newspaper and thought, "We've met before."

I bolted the attic steps two at a time and located the box where the residue of my college years had settled in sedimentary layers. Like an archeologist on a bone I located the photographs and spread them across the floor.

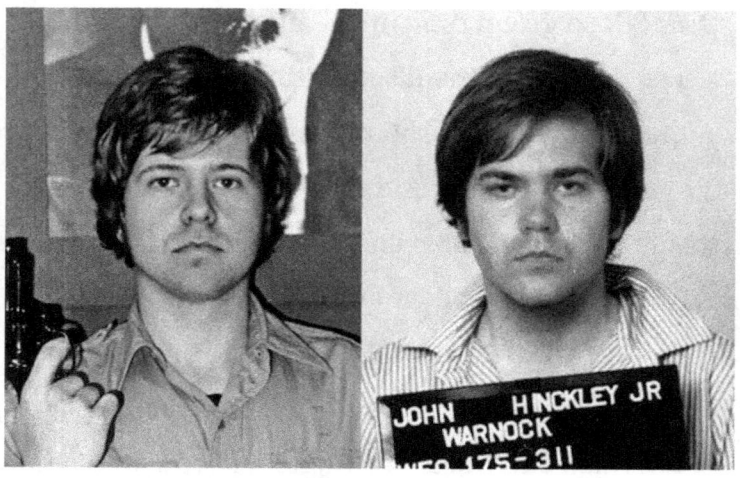

The similarities were unmistakable despite a six-year lapse between photographs. The downturned corners of his mouth, the cupid's bow of his upper lip, the narrow bridge, ball and nostril flare of his nose, the bend of his eyebrows, the curl of his sideburns around the base of his ears, even the blemishes on his neck and cheeks, all mirrored the images of Hinckley assembled by *The Times*. When combined with the article linking Hinckley to Frank Collin and the Chicago NSPA, I was convinced I had hit the photojournalism jackpot.

I glanced up to find my fiancé Caroline looking over my shoulder and realized that in the countless hours we'd spent getting to know each other I had neglected to mention my infiltration of the American Nazi Party. The iconic Nazi images spread across the attic floor combined with the *New York Times* headlines about the Reagan shooting had her wondering who the hell she was about to marry. Clearly Caroline did not share my enthusiastic response to discovering I was somehow connected to the attempted assassination of the President of the United States.

Hours after my epiphany in the attic I met with editors at the *New York Daily News*, *United Press*, and *TIME Magazine*, before eventually striking the midnight deal with the *New York Post*. I later signed with Outline, a photo agency anxious to represent my images in Europe and negotiations in Paris, Munich, Milan, London and half a dozen other European markets followed.

The struggle to uncover the truth became paramount after false Hinckley images surfaced, making media outlets reluctant to publish unsubstantiated photographs. *American Photographer* magazine wrote,

> Following the attempted assassination of President Reagan, and the ensuing scramble for Hinckley photos, many magazines and newspapers ran pictures that turned out to be frauds.
>
> Outline, the photo agency representing Carter ... made "an unusual deal" in selling the photos to Time, Paris Match, Bunte, Gente, and the London Daily Mirror, even though their editors are not able to publish them unless it is proven that their subject is truly Hinckley.[2]

Over the next two months I engaged in a series of exchanges with the FBI and the prosecuting District Attorney. More than once I felt the tap of paranoia on my shoulder. After all, I was raised on a steady diet of conspiracy theories surrounding the assassination of John F. Kennedy, which coincidentally occurred on my birthday. Government lies and CIA manipulation of the press had been well documented through disclosures about the Pentagon Papers and Operation Mockingbird. As I looked into the faces of the Nazis inhabiting my photo essay, I couldn't help but wonder if there might be a real-life Manchurian Candidate staring back.

Ronald Reagan recovered from the assassination attempt and went on to complete two full terms as President. James Brady struggled with his injury for the remainder of his life and died in 2014. His death was ruled a homicide as a result of the wounds he sustained during the assassination attempt, but prosecutors elected not to press murder charges against Hinckley. In 1982 John W. Hinckley Jr. was found innocent by reason of insanity and spent 35 years in a psychiatric hospital.

I still don't know if the man I met in the Chicago Nazi Party headquarters was the man responsible for the murder of James Brady and the attempted assassination of President Reagan, but a document I recently obtained through the Freedom of Information Act has confirmed that in April 1981 the Director of the FBI received a request to "perform a full photographic comparison of these photos with photos of subject John Warnock Hinckley, Jr.". To this day the agency has remained silent on the results of their investigation and the man's true identity remains publicly unknown.

*****

Today

The recent rise of the "alt-right" movement and the violence that erupted in Charlottesville, Virginia has rekindled interest in my decades-old encounter with the American Nazi Party and the fruitless search for truth that followed.

What is more dangerous, the racial contempt displayed by a small group of white supremacists in Chicago or Charlottesville, or the implicit encouragement of an administration that emboldens people of hate to act against people of color? I have stood toe to toe with the pistol-toting, swastika-wearing variety of racism and from my perspective the inflammatory rhetoric of those in power, cloaked in Orwellian doublespeak and designed to fuel the cultural resentments buried in our national psyche, is far more dangerous. Racism, which was once secretly concealed beneath America's thin white skin, is now blatantly displayed on our inflamed red necks.

When "alt-right" ideology becomes mainstream and "alternative truth" competes with "objective truth" for the attention of our nation, it's time to look back and examine the road that got us here, a road that passed through Selma in the sixties, Chicago in the seventies, and now passes through Washington D.C. When America comes to the next fork in that road the direction we choose depends on the strength of our people to see through the artifice, obfuscation and misdirection of those trying to alter what is real.

Pulitzer Prize winning author Thomas E. Ricks wrote, "The struggle to see things as they are is perhaps the fundamental driver of Western civilization ... It is the agreement that objective reality exists, that people of goodwill can perceive it, and that other people will change their views when presented with the facts of the matter."[4]

Meanwhile, Big Brother is watching.

[1] FEDS SEIZE NAZI PIX (May 29, 1981) New York Post, 1

[2] IN CAMERA (Sept. 1981) American Photographer, 10

[3] King, W. (April 13, 1981) Hinckley Inquiry Studies Alleged Nazi 'Flirtation', The New York Times, 20

[4] Ricks, T. E. (2017) Churchill & Orwell The Fight For Freedom, 270

Don Carter

Don Carter is a sommelier, wine educator and writer. His humorous, educational writing platform is called *WineSnark, The Wise-Ass Guide to Wine Appreciation*. After 25 years in the wine trade it's safe to say that wine gives Don's life meaning. It's the reason he gets out of bed every afternoon.

Recently Don ventured out of his wine writing comfort zone and began writing personal memoirs. And why not? When your personal memoirs involve murder, a presidential assassination attempt and infiltration of the American Nazi Party, why not share it with the world. After all, it's a lot more interesting than telling people that Chardonnay tastes better with chicken.

You can find Don's other work at Winesnark.com

A Silent Victory
By Patricia Lee

Carpow, Roman Scotland, 185 AD.

Corellia felt a sharp jab in her side. "Get out there!" cursed Fabious, her slave owner, "The best pickings'll be gone!"

Resistance or even protest was pointless. Prising herself away from the pile of oysters she was opening, Corellia wiped her salty hands on her gown and flicked her copper hair from her eyes.

"Go!" he bellowed again, shoving his massive fist into her young, strong back as he shoved her out the hut door. Corellia stumbled against the roughly hewn doorjamb, bruising her arm. Gathering her skirts, she ran.

Puddles from recent rain splashed her white legs and soaked her hob-nailed boots, loot from an earlier expedition. She had given no thought to the Roman legionary she'd wrenched them from. He was dead. She wondered how many would be dead today.

A battle had been raging all morning in the ploughed field between their village and the Roman fort. The fort's neat stone wall jutted out arrogantly separating Roman territory from Barbaricum. She snorted as the word entered her head. It was the Romans who lived ate and breathed Barbaricum: what could be more barbaric than legion fighting legion? Brave men slaughtered by their own brothers-in-arms?

Flinging herself into the muddy field, she hitched her skirts around her hips and began to pick her way forward. The field smelt of blood, animal manure and fear. Like debris washed onto a beach, prone men were everywhere, lying as they had fallen. Pila stuck out of them like bulrush spears in a bog. Around them, the red puddles became pitted with holes as the rain began; torrents of tears for the sheer obscene waste of it all.

Lifting the first man's arm, she avoided his glazed eyes, still open with horror and searched for a bronze purse on his muddy wrist. Finding one and forcing it open, she found only an as, a Roman penny. Seeing bright metal under him, she dragged out his dagger and went in search of better plunder.

She was a slight woman, although long hours of physical labour on the farm had made her strong, so some of the soldier's bodies proved too awkward for her to move from hideous stacks four or five high. Instead she sought out the single corpses whose last possessions were easier to rifle.

Already others from the village had joined her in a

frenzy of greed tempered with caution, for they all watched the fort warily in case the victorious soldiers came out and attacked them for desecrating bodies.

For half an hour, Corellia unbuckled scabbards and cuirasses finding only a few sesterces to gild the brutal fumbling of her fingers.

Then she heard a moan.

For a moment she thought it was herself regretting the thwarted beauty of the young soldier's face she beheld at her feet, his once perfect features smeared with blood and mud. She held herself still and listened, her chest now tight with emotion. It was a dirty errand Fabious had sent her on; she'd rather muck out the pigs than this. She bit her lip to prevent salty tears and hitched up her skirts and her resolve. So much beauty was lost here, but she had a job to do.

Before she moved on, she leant down and raised the young soldier's face to her own, brushing his mouth with her cheek to feel for his breath, believing her warm presence alone might restore life. However, it was hopeless. She felt no warmth there. He was cold, very cold from the rain. His spirit had already sailed with the tide on the ocean of death.

Suddenly Tadia, the village herbalist, screamed out to all the looters, "The soldiers are coming! Go back now!" she warned Corellia, scrambling away laden with soldiers' belongings.

Corellia sprang to her feet but tripped heavily. She had caught her foot on something. Twisting around, she grabbed at the obstruction.

Around her ankle was a human hand!

The young soldier was not yet dead!

Almost immediately his hand lost its grip. A final desperate gesture?

Whispering to the soldier, she covered his face with his shield. Soon the soldiers would be upon her so she turned and fled.

Slowed by the mud they did not catch her. She ran into the welcoming green of the forest. They called out to her in their frustration, threatening acts of depravity.

Panting under a brambleberry, she listened until the men's voices dimmed. At least Fabious would not beat her, for she held tightly a few stolen sesterces. She still had the dagger. True to the soldiers' pattern, they would return tomorrow to collect the dead and dump them in a large nameless pit, burying the mutiny forever. She would regret the young, beautiful soldier who died reaching out to her He alone retained some humanity amongst the piles of bone and skin left in the field.

Returning to the hut, she dutifully dropped the coins on

the table and washed her face and hands in a copper bowl near the door. Fabious and his wife, Aelia, were out. The rain ceased and it was almost dark. She was very tired and ready for rest in the tiny room she occupied next to the pigsty. Before reaching the hut, she heard a fragile moan carried to her on the evening wind. Could the young soldier really still be alive?

She slapped tiredness from her face. She had to know if he was really dead.

In the waistband of her shapeless gallic shift was the stolen soldier's dagger. She touched its hilt which stilled her trembling and gave her confidence to face the ghosts of the battlefield. She prayed quickly to Fortuna, holding the medal of the goddess which hung around her neck, "Goddess, keep me safe."

Retracing her steps, she skirted corpses whose ghastly white faces reflected in the moonlight. Squinting her eyes in the gloom she sought the inverted shield she'd placed over the young soldier's face to protect him from crows and the weather. But every dead soldier seemed to have a shield. One by one, she watched for movement. Soon it would be completely dark and she would have to return. Searching wearily now, she checked a few more bodies until the fear and uncertainty of her search made her turn back.

Again, she heard the moan.

It came, wrenched out of the deepest hopelessness and pain. Changing direction, she advanced towards the sound.

Moonlight glinted on a shield. Yes! There he was! Under it the young man's face was covered in mud. She wiped the muck away with her shift and placing a finger near his nostrils felt for breath. Holding her own, she detected a very faint movement of warm air.

He was alive!

But what was she to do? She could not lift him, certainly not covered as he was in heavy armour.

Awkwardly she unstrapped his leather cuirass. The heavy, metal-studded leather kilt came off next. Under it his woollen tunic was thin and sticky. What Corellia needed was a cart for he was too heavy for her to drag any distance. She remembered, Fabious kept a handcart in the yard behind the pigsty.

Returning to the farm, she immediately dropped down on all fours hearing her employers moving inside the hut readying themselves for bed. She edged round and slipped in the gate of the sty. The pigs thought she was there to feed them and started grunting. She stopped until they settled. Reaching out, she grabbed the cart. Its axle squeaked sharply but a little mud deadened the sound as she pulled it back to the field.

Years later she would wonder how she managed to roll

the young soldier onto the cart and pull him through the mud and ruts. At the forest's edge her knotted shoulders and back spasmed as she dropped to the ground.

Gasping for breath, she forced her stiff arms to move again. Getting the soldier to good shelter was beyond her. A handcart cannot be pulled through a pathless forest. Fifty yards into the forest was the brambleberry under which she had already sheltered. It would have to do. She managed to get the cart near to it and dragged him the rest of the way. Covering him with his shield and piles of leaves, she hid his helmet and the leather kilt in a hole, covering all over with bracken fronds.

She did not have the strength to fetch him water. Her first priority was to drag the cart back because its disappearance would only arouse suspicion. "Stay well," she whispered over him and placed the medal of Fortuna on his chest.

Back in her simple room, Corellia fell immediately into a weary sleep.

***

As usual the screams of Aelia woke her in the morning: "Get up! The cow wants milking and Fabious needs more eggs to take to the market," she whined. "He is bringing the whip now."

Raising her weak and stiffened body, Corellia pulled

open the door and dragged herself up. Aelia enjoyed wielding the whip herself and today she brought the knotted thong down on Corellia's back. "Ha!' she crowed, "I have it already!"

Corellia struggled to her feet defending her face from further attack and began her laborious tasks. She collected all but one freshly laid egg which she hid down among the nesting straw and also managed to hide a pitcher of milk on a rafter in the cowshed. It was the first milking and contained the most cream.

With Fabious at the market and Aelia visiting Tadia for yet another remedy for indigestion, Corellia slipped away into the forest. Its green shroud enveloped her. In the pitcher of milk she had beaten the fresh egg and in another carried water soured with vinegar to bathe the soldier's wounds. Fearful of what she might find, she parted the brambles and flattened them down with her boots. Under the battered red and gold shield, the young man lay deeply asleep. Dark brows and black hair emphasised his pale, almost grey, skin. She touched his cheek with her hand. Today his skin was slightly warmer. Raising his head, she brought the pitcher to his lips. Only a little went down. She studied his torso for injury and found a patch on his side sticky with bright blood. Ripping the tunic, a weeping sword wound was exposed just above the second last rib.

She bathed away the congealed blood and staunched the fresh flow with a wad of old cloth brought for the purpose. She bandaged the wound, using his arm pressed down to help stop the bleeding. She did not know what to do about the huge lump on his head so she left it alone.

Again she tried the milk. He swallowed very little. Tears of frustration stung her eyes. She was risking her life to tend him and yet there seemed little hope. Tomorrow, she would bring a spade to bury him.

Taking heavier branches she made a better camouflage, as artless as possible, to feign nature and interlaced it with more bracken. At the last moment, she left the pitcher, knowing as surely as the sun would rise in the morning the milk would sour before he could lift it to drink.

On her way back to the farm, she saw in the distance men loading carts with bodies for burial. This was why she had retrieved his shield and cuirass and buried the rest in case anyone wondered where the body belonging to them had gone.

For the rest of the day she spun wool for the mistress, scoured pots and cooked a late afternoon meal while her mind worried about the soldier. As a mutineer, his life was forfeit if he was seen again by legionaries in the camp. Large numbers of soldiers roamed in detachments throughout the day to and from the port. Only disguised as a native Briton would he be able to move anywhere if he recovered. Anyone helping a suspected enemy of the 'Senate and People of Rome', if not a citizen, was subject to death without trial and Corellia was not a citizen.

Sanctuary within easy travelling distance must soon be found for him. Without proper shelter he would soon die as winter closed in. She helped him in the snatches of time when her slave owners were absent. They had already been out twice in two days and were unlikely to go out again soon, being both incredibly lazy. Without her slave collar, long ago she would have fled from them back to her own people beyond the Roman frontier. But the slave collar marked her as a runaway whose recapture meant a whipping and mutilation too horrible to imagine.

It was almost sunset when she remembered a favourite little known spot of Tadia's. It was a secluded place near a hidden spring once sacred to the Druids long before the arrival of conquering Romans. She had helped the old woman gather mistletoe there from the ancient oaks. One had a trunk with a girth greater than the total of three people's arm spans. Struck by lightning long ago, the hollow had burnt out forming a concealed space. The soldier could shelter there if she blocked off the entrance with branches so no wild boar could reach him. It was a plan but it filled her with despair. How could she transport the dead weight of a sick man over such a distance?

Sneaking out with a small olive oil lamp long after Fabious and his wife were asleep, she went to the soldier and uncovered him in his prickly nest. She was surprised to find the milk all gone. Yet, as he was still unconscious how was she to drag him the great distance to the old tree? If only he woke, perhaps he could crawl or stagger against her some of the way?

She washed his face with water and slapped one cheek with her open palm. A red welt appeared and he murmured. Dark shadows ringed his eyes and his face felt hot with sweat beaded on his forehead. Corellia checked his wound and repacked it with clean linen but for a battlefield fever she had no remedy. If she left him here again tomorrow what if he became delirious and cried out? She remembered a sleeping potion used by mothers to soothe troubled children but daring not ask Tadia for it, she searched for the plant herself. This simple plan took many hours to complete. Without rest, she began construction of a litter and two hours before daybreak rolled the soldier onto it. Tired but determined, she hauled it deeper into the forest and left him under a spreading tree. Carefully she replaced the shield over his face and again covered the litter with branches and leaves.

***

By dawn with her strength almost gone, she crept back to her den and to Aelia standing by the door, "And where have you been?" she accused.

"I went to relieve myself, mistress."

"I hope so," said the woman, but her eyes narrowed, "now get and milk the cow."

This time the whip caught her across the neck and the lacerations dripped with blood as Corellia staggered to the cowshed fumbling for the bucket.

As she milked, Aelia scowled, "Yesterday's milk had no cream. I'll wait here until you finish that pail or there'll be no butter for the bread today!"

When Corellia brought her the pail, Aelia said, "You better look lively all day or I'll send Fabious with the whip."

"I am not well," pleaded Corellia.

"I'll have none of that. A slave cannot be ill." She pranced off with the full bucket.

Corellia slept in snatches whenever Aelia lifted her eyes from her which was not often enough. Come night she expected to lay down for a nap and rise with the moon but her body refused to follow her brain's clock and it was dawn before she woke.

All morning she was in a panic: 'He has no water!' 'He might wake and wander off into the forest!' She fretted like a kind-hearted child with an injured bird. He would die without her.

"I will fetch wood from the forest," she suggested at midday but Aelia shook her head.

"We do not need wood, slave," she sneered, "go tend the pigs."

They kept her working late that night and she remembered the unknown soldier's dagger hidden under her palliasse; yet to kill was as foreign to her as it was to leave someone to die alone in a cold, muddy field.

***

So it was hours after dark before she arrived to succour him. Because the moon was hidden behind thick grey clouds she did not see, at first, his eyes looking at her. When she lifted his head to drink, he took her hand and kissed it and she was so startled she dropped the bowl and had to refill it.

"Thank you," he said when she gave him the second drink. He lay down again, his face creased with pain. She leant near him and asked if he could move.

"I will try," he whispered but the pain was overwhelming and he slumped again.

"There is a place with water," she coaxed, "you will be safe there if we can reach it."

"I don't know." His voice was weary.

Eventually, he sat up and held his head in his hands for

a long time. She felt guilty at the tremendous effort it took him.

She explained, "I am a slave. For two nights I have carried and dragged you here. All day I work for the master and mistress. They whip me if I am slow. Please, you must try."

They struggled their way through the forest. His legs were sound but he staggered from pain and every time he fell, she felt her soul go out to him in despair. She carried him against her together with the shield and a loaf of bread. If she died at the base of the ancient oak, she would get him there.

Spent beyond exhaustion, before dawn they reached the hidden spring. For a long time they sat unable to speak.

"Where is the oak?" he asked.

"It is there," she pointed, "at the edge of the glade."

"I will get there and hide. You must go."

"No, let me help you there first."

He raised his chin wearily, "I will not have them whip you for me. Go and rest. I will make the bread last two days."

Cupping her hands, she drank from the spring and left.

***

When Aelia discovered the flat loaf missing her face turned purple. Corellia backed against the hut wall, "I dropped it in the mud," she explained, "and had to feed it to the pigs."

"Imbecile, it was a gift for Tadia, to pay for the medicine."

"What is the herb she gives you? I will find it and prepare it for nothing."

Aelia described the herb and said, "Go but if you return without it, no food for you!"

Scouring the edges of the forest, it was some hours before she found the herb and picked it. Clumsy with weariness, when she turned her foot caught in a bramble cane and she fell down to the ground. Bruised and in shock, exhaustion from all her exertions overwhelmed her and she fell asleep. It was already night when she woke and limped back to the hut.

Aelia was livid and Fabious brooded menacingly in the corner, "What is it in the forest which delays you?" he demanded.

Turning to Corellia she said, "You have a lover, don't you?"

Nothing Corellia said could convince them otherwise. So at night, they manacled her in the hut.

She knew now what she must do at the first opportunity. But Fabious watched her in the morning with his puffy eyes and when he tired Aelia took over, peering at her with a steely gaze.

***

There was no chance to escape the next day or the one after. 'He will be starving by now and his wound putrid.' The handsome young man would die because of Aelia and her fat husband.

Yet on the third day came her chance. They were lazy. Fabious took his eyes off her to find a rock to throw at a pig and she streaked away and jumped behind the pigsty. When he rose and shouted, she already had the soldier's dagger and was running towards the other huts in the village. Diving under the nearest neighbour's wooden granary, she lay concealed until darkness fell, her shawl pulled around her. Though Fabious and his friends searched for her, believing her to have run further than she had, they looked in all the wrong places. Aelia's frustrated squeals amused her and if she hadn't been afraid of discovery and its gruesome consequences, she might have laughed.

When rats began to scurry over her feet in the darkness, she reached up with the dagger and finding a knot hole in the wooden floor poked into the food store and half-filled an empty sack with grain. From a hut whose owner had no dog, she stole a man's shift and cape and an old cooking pot someone's child had abandoned in the dirt.

In the forest, the way so painfully learnt three nights before came more easily. In the moonlight, her copper hair glinted as she ran.

Sitting beside the spring to catch her breath, she wondered what she would find. Moving across the glade she peered, looking for a slumped-down figure, cold and stiff. She already tasted the bitterness in her mouth.

At the tree's dark cavern, she sucked in her breath and reached slowly into the blackness: the moment became a gateway which Fortuna might open or shut as She willed.

He took her hand and she gasped as he pulled her in.

"Where have you been?" he asked, his face close to hers and his breath warm on her neck.

"Suspicious, they chained me at night."

He felt the lacerations the manacles had made on her wrists and gently brushed them with his mouth. "I escaped today," she continued," and have been hiding."

"You cannot return."

He pulled her down so she was sitting and she noticed his arm was no longer bandaged to his side.

"Are you well?"

"I am better. The blow to my head is worst. I have kept the sword wound clean. Have you food?"

"I'm sorry, only grains."

One of his arms circled her waist and with the other

hand, he brushed the hair from her face, "Why did you save me?" he asked.

She shook her head unable to put into words her actions.

"What is your name?" she asked.

"It is Victorianus... no name for a shamed soldier. I will change it. What is yours?"

"Corellia."

"Corellia," he repeated the name as if tasting it.

"It is a slave name,' she confessed, "I cannot remember any other."

"You will get a new name tonight too." He thought deeply for a few minutes and then said, "I will call you Victoria -she who triumphs over death." And he placed the necklace with Fortuna's medal back around her neck.

He lifted her chin and kissed the running tears. Through the night they did not loose arms from each other.

In the morning, he took the dagger and removed the rivet in her collar. They buried the shield and collar behind the ancient oak and left the grove. He was now a young dark-haired Briton in his gallic shift and she a freewoman in her torn gown and shawl. With the sack of grain and the dagger they began their long, slow journey through the forest and before the weather turned to winter, they journeyed to find a settlement far from Carpow.

Patricia Lee

Patricia Lee is a semi-retired English teacher living on a small farm in the idyllic Southern Highlands of NSW, Australia which she shares with her husband and youngest son. A love of history and the natural environment underpins her novels, short stories and poetry. Her particular historical interest is Roman Britain, a past in which she believes her antecedents lived their lives with the same aspirations as those we have today- freedom, love and fulfillment.

Her published works include a young adult novel *'History at my Fingertips'*, with stories and poems included in numerous newsletters and anthologies. Her best work she believes, two 'Roman' novels, are yet to be published. She is currently working on a novel set in rural Australia and a collection of her poetry and art.

As well as writing fiction and poetry, Patricia recounts amusing episodes raising ducks, chickens and turkeys in her blog: amundr@wordpress.com

Attack of the Communist-Hordes
By Brad Bennett

A frantic announcer suddenly interrupted the scratchy music emanating from the small transistor radio! ...

"SHOTS FIRED! SHOTS FIRED!"

The woman sitting across from me was busy at her filing cabinet she seemed not to hear.

I strained to hear the man's frantic voice..."Multiple gunshots fired at the presidential motor...."

The announcer's voice was breaking up. I couldn't make out the words.

"Turn it up!" I asked.

But the woman ignored me... more undecipherable scratchy noises continued from its tiny speaker. "Did you hear that?" I asked as she turned around in her chair.

"Oh, probably some robbery is going on somewhere." She answered. "Here's you're approved application. Just sign it. That's all I need."

I thanked her and scribbled my name on the papers.

I was at the Air Force Base Credit Union during my lunch break. I had applied for a used car loan, now my time was up, and I had to return to my workstation near the flight line.

The air outside was turning cold. I zipped up my light

flight jacket and began walking back. I didn't know it then, but I was about to enter one of my strangest experiences ever as an airman in the US Air Force.

The North Texas Panhandle was the site of one of the largest military airbases in the world. Parked along its huge three-mile long runway, were dozens of nuclear weapon-carrying B52 bombers. It was known as Amarillo Air Force Base.

There are many panhandles in the USA, but the North Texas panhandle is the most well known, probably because Texas is the state that always leans towards the extreme. For instance, there's a Cadillac graveyard there, with discarded Caddie's half-buried in the sand. It's an art statement. Other than that, there's not much up there to see except prairie dogs, longhorn cattle, and miles of endless bald prairie. And of course, like anywhere in Texas, good old boys and a few good old gals.

This was where I found myself stationed after Basic Training in San Antonio. The Air base was about 10 miles east of the city of Amarillo. At that time, the city had a population of only 100,000, while the base itself had close to 130,000. Of course, this creates a big problem, not many of those good old gals to go around.

This area of Texas is as flat as a pool table, stretching for hundreds of miles in every direction. Anyone stationed there would immediately get the running joke when they arrived. "Don't even think of going AWOL," they'd say. "The military police can still see you three days later."

As far as sightseeing goes, that honor went to a single tree standing by the famous Route 66 highway that ran by the base. That tree held the distinction of being the only tree along that route for over eighty miles. People used to stop by just to have their picture taken next to it. Yet despite it being the only tree there, some fool still managed to run off the road and hit it.

But the biggest event on that base was when a Red Alert practice was on.

Those cigar-shaped B52 Stratofortress bombers were scrambled immediately--one directly behind the other. The noise would become a thunderous roar, as they formed an endless chain of flaming silver birds across the Texas sky

There's also a sizable population of Texas-size jackrabbits living out near the runway. By coincidence, after each of these Red Alerts, the chow hall menu would feature southern-fried rabbit, a little stringy, but not bad.

Amarillo Airbase was a SAC base (Strategic Air Command.) And these mighty aircraft were part of the command's mission to be a deterrent to the threat of the Soviet Union's nuclear arsenal. The big planes were stationed in this remote area to be safely launched before the Soviet Union could react.

The base also was the headquarters of the Air Training Command, and that's why I was there. I was assigned work at the art studio near the flight line, as a graphic artist. My job was to produce graphic safety posters, and jet mechanics maintenance illustrated drawings to instruct ground personnel. It was a challenging, rewarding job. It also offered me the opportunity to have my own cartoon strip, which was printed in the base newspaper. It was called "Rex Riley." An ex-fighter pilot supplied the writing. The name was his sobriquet for careless pilots. During this tough old veterans career he had witnessed every mishap a pilot could get into--a significant problem the Air Force had at that time.

My pilot-writer would provide the safety issues, and then I would go out poking around on the flight line, sketching the aircraft in question. Safety was certainly something I had to learn. I was just a dumbass kid fresh off the farm, now here I was straying around in this dangerous environment drawing pictures. I was soon made aware of the horrible incidences that took place around me. One ground worker was actually sucked into a jet intake. Another was killed, when he walked into a whirling prop. This area was no place to stroll around carelessly.

After a year there, I had finally accumulated enough time to go home on leave. I decided I would buy a car and drive it back to my home in Oregon. That's why I found myself at the Credit Union on a day that no one would ever forget. That day was November 22, 1963.

When I returned to the studio from the credit union, I was immediately surprised to see everybody scurrying around in panic. I spotted my section boss talking with a group of people. He saw me and quickly came over.

"There's a troop truck outside." He said. "Better get your self on it. No time to talk now. You'll be briefed at the Air Police Headquarters!"

"Why? What's going on?"

"Haven't you heard? President Kennedy's been SHOT! We're in a state of emergency."

"Shot, oh my god!" I stammered. "But why Air Police? I'm an illustrator, not a security guy?"

"I know," he quickly replied. "It's not just you. Hell, everybody's going!"

I headed immediately for the door. Outside I spotted the blue flatbed truck with airmen of every enlisted rank climbing on to it. I went over and hopped on.

As we drove through the base, I could hear the thunder of the B 52 engines roaring up. A Red Alert was on! 'Oh,

God!' I thought. Is this the real thing?

When we arrived at the Air Police HQ, we were quickly ordered off the truck, and directed to the main building. Inside we were joined up with more men into a wide briefing area. Soon a nervous-looking officer stood before us. He called for our attention. "Please be ADVISED!" he announced loudly. "This airbase is now under Full DefCon 1 Alert!" I wondered what the hell that meant?

He paused for dramatic effect. "There has been a hostile threat against our nation from unknown, alien forces." He stopped again to emphasize the seriousness of that statement. You are NOW!" he went on. "Charged with protecting the property of the United States Air Force. You will each be assigned to secure a perimeter around valuable sensitive military installations." He paused again. "The safety of this base is paramount. Do you understand?"

Then he abruptly turned and left out the side door. That was it? No more information? We were left standing there completely dumbfounded.

Then another officer appeared and quickly ordered us into a staging area outside an armory door. Once there, several Air Policemen began distributing M1 Carbines to each of us from the storeroom.

"Where's the bullets?" a man ahead of me asked the guard.

"We were told not to issue ammo." The policeman answered. "Just act as if it's loaded."

"What then?" The guy replied. "Is the enemy going to act like they're shot?"

Nervous laughter filled the room.

When the policeman handed me my weapon, I looked at him for some possible reasoning--he looked away. He was probably just as perplexed as we were. Next, we were herded back outside and ordered into more waiting trucks, then we proceeded in the direction of the flight line. It was clear to me now; I would be guarding one of the B 52's.

When we entered through the guardhouse gate at the runway, two police guards appeared. One of the men was leading a huge German Sheppard. When the dog spotted us in the back of that truck, he went berserk! He reared up and charged at us snarling viciously, dragging the dog's handler behind him. The guard fought to contain the powerful animal, its snapping teeth only inches from our faces. The other man quickly joined him to hold the beast back.

We then proceeded on through the gate, shaking in our boots. It was painfully obvious, if they hadn't held that dog back, we would've been torn to pieces!

This whole thing now was starting to look damn scary. We were rushing down a long runway in the back of an open truck, with a freezing December wind biting into our faces. All I was wearing was light khaki clothing and jacket. I had on low cut office shoes, with no gloves or proper hat. My hands were starting to freeze up. I could barely hold the carbine. On top of that, I had no idea what was happening? Was the president dead, and the base about to be invaded? Were those departing B-52 bombers now dropping nuclear bombs on Moscow?

Are we now in a full-scale nuclear war?

My mind was racing wildly as we proceeded down the flight line. Up ahead, I could see about half of the main force of B52's still remaining. This was standard practice; the base always kept half its strength back in reserve in case a second strike was needed. By now I was starting to get so cold, I didn't care.

The truck stopped at the first bomber, the officer in the cab came around and ordered the first man out. Then we proceeded on to the next plane. Finally, my B 52 came up. I awkwardly stumbled my way off the back. The truck sped off into the distance, leaving me standing there in front of the menacing airplane wondering what to do? Where should I stand guard, I received no training in this? Besides, my hands were so numb; I couldn't use my weapon even if it was loaded.

Finally, I decided to hell with this. I went over and leaned into the shelter of one of the big wheels. I propped up the gun on the strut and put my freezing hands in my coat pockets. The light soon began to fade as the sun sank lower over the western horizon. The more it disappeared, the colder and lonelier I got, my shivering only adding to my misery. The wind whistling through the prairie grass seemed to add even more starkness to the whole eerie scene. I gazed down the flight line to see if I could make out the other parked bombers. But they were spaced out over quite a distance; I could barely make them out.

I felt totally helpless out there with nothing but an empty gun, guarding enough nuclear weapons to destroy half of Texas, most of Oklahoma, and parts of Kansas thrown in.

It was getting completely dark now. I started thinking about what the officer had said..."Our nation is under a serious threat from outside forces!"

What did he mean by that? Was there a gang of communist hordes out there hiding in the prairie grass? Every sound I could hear in the dark was beginning to stir up fears in my imagination. I'm a sitting duck out here I thought. I couldn't even fight off one freaking jackrabbit, let alone an attack of Red insurgents. I decided it best to get out of this freezing wind. I climbed up into the big jets wheel-well opening like some nocturnal desert critter scurrying into its burrow.

It was pitch black up in the wheel compartment, but somehow, I found a position among the hydraulic lines and steel fittings. I curled up into a ball, trying to get as comfortable as I could. If the Communist hordes came now and blew up the jet, I would at least go out of this world warm!

Soon I drifted off.

A ROAR of a jet engine suddenly jolted me awake! Oh, my God! The B 52 is taking off!

I jumped back down the landing strut in sheer panic, banging my arms and legs against steel objects as I fell-- hitting the tarmac in a jumbled heap. I got up--looked around--nobody was there? In the distance, I could see the flame of a fighter jet climbing away from the runway. I felt like a complete moron!

I don't think I was asleep in that wheel well, but in some sort of cold storage trance. I rubbed my sore, aching body from my sorry escape from the bomber. Off to the horizon, I could see streaks of orange-yellow glowing in the eastern sky. It was now early morning. The bastards had forgotten about us and left us out here all night!

I don't know what time it must have been when the blue truck finally pulled up to my position. I was so cold and stiff; I could barely climb up on to it. The driver slammed it in gear, and we rolled off to the next B 52. It seemed to take forever as we stopped for each plane, as each poor shivering devil, like me, struggled to get on.

The ride back to the Air Police building was worse. The driver must have thought it would be more humane, if he drove as fast as he could. The cold wind whipping at us at 70 miles per hour in the back of an open vehicle was like being dipped in ice water!

Once we arrived at the gate, the police dog tried to attack us again!

Over the next few weeks, we learned of the Kennedy assassination just like everyone else. No conspiracy or evil plot against America. No communist hordes were going to attack us; only one lone gunman named Oswald had caused all that grief.

Not long ago, my wife and I were driving up to LA from San Diego in our RV. We passed a sign along the route that declared: See the great aircraft from the past. Visit The Las Angeles Outdoor Air Museum--2 miles ahead!

So, we pulled in to take a tour. While we were strolling among the antique relics, we came across a man about my age working on the aircraft. I introduced myself and told him about my time working around these same aircraft. He was amazed at my story; he mentioned he was in the Air Force at that time. As we talked, I noticed we were standing near an abandoned B-52. This got me to thinking about the

Red Alert during Kennedy's assassination. I asked him if he was involved in that alert too?

"Oh, yes!" he told me. "I was stationed here in California at Andrews Air Force base. We were all rounded up and sent out to the flight line to guard the aircraft.

"No, kidding? Me too!" I replied.

"But you know what was a damnedest thing?" he added. "They gave us guns, but no damn bullets!"

Brad Bennett

Brad lives with his wife, Norrie, in Oliver BC, "Canada's Wine Capital" in the heart of the Okanagan Valley. Since retiring Brad and Norrie have enjoyed the pastoral beauty and friendly existence the area offers. They love having children and grandchildren visit from the Coast. Norrie enjoys touring the vineyards and shopping the local farm markets. When Brad is not playing pool or doing crosswords, he is avidly pursuing his lifelong dream of writing short stories, fiction and non-fiction, by reflecting on life through past encounters.

Brad was born in Oregon and happily roamed the forests growing up. After his stint in the U.S. Air Force as a freelance graphic designer in Dallas Texas, he immigrated to Canada in 1977. Before setting up his own advertising design studio, he was an ad agency creative director in both Calgary and Vancouver, working on major Canadian accounts.

For a writer's work to be chosen by Living Springs for publication in *Stories Through the Ages* is truly an honor. He is ecstatic and very thankful for the opportunity.

Your Mother's Sock
By Elizabeth Bobst

Just as Cora opened the microwave door to pop in a Tupperware bowl filled with last night's leftovers, her phone rang. She closed the door firmly and hit the quick heat button three times in rapid succession before she turned to pick up the phone. Squinting to see the writing that she was too vain to enlarge on her iPhone screen, she moved the phone further away to see if that helped bring the tiny letters into focus. It did. Her dad was calling. She groaned and reached for the glass of red wine she'd been sipping slowly for the past hour, ever since her husband and son had texted to say they'd be home late. Cora drained it before she tapped the screen to answer the call.

"Hi, Dad," she said brightly, her voice sounding forced and fake in her own ear. She knew from experience that the wrong tone of voice would immediately send the conversation in a bad direction. She looked longingly at her dinner spinning around in the mysteriously muted light inside the microwave. She quickly looked away, wondering if she was slowly killing herself by just looking at the microwaved food, much less eating it.

"I *have* to find another place to live." Her dad's voice, a booming bass still commanding at eighty-four, drilled deep through her ear, along the well-worn pathway into her brain where his anger exploded, lighting up all her familiar alert centers.

"What happened?" Her stomach clenched as she walked out of the kitchen and around the corner into the laundry room, her need to move suddenly urgent. Facing the dryer, she pulled the phone away from her ear, tapped the speaker button, and laid the phone down on the tiled countertop. After pulling open the dryer door, she stuck her hand into the jumble of warm clothes to check their level of dryness.

"This place is *riddled* with incompetents. Not *one* of them can do *anything* right!" He sounded further away or speaker phone, which enabled her to take a deeper breath as she pulled out a pair of pants and shook them quietly, not wanting him to know he didn't have her full attention. She smoothed the pants out straight and laid them flat on the counter. She assumed he was talking about the CNAs at the assisted living place he and her mother had recently moved into together. He called the Certified Nursing Assistants "helpers," and he didn't like many of them. On his good days, he accused them of treating him like an old person and doing his thinking for him. On his bad days, he accused them of being racist and trying to stick it to the white man. Cora didn't yet know what kind of a day today was.

He continued. "Today, they lost your mother's sock!"

She hesitated, pulled out a t-shirt from the dryer and laid it on the counter to fold it, and then asked cautiously, "How did they lose her sock?"

Her parents had transitioned into assisted living from their independent living apartment two months previously, when her dad had broken his foot and could no longer care for her mother, whose dementia had slowly worsened. He had prided himself on the care he was able to give his wife and breaking his foot had taken away many facets of his independence, including driving. But the most difficult transition was accepting help from the people who were there to help them. His constant anger and criticism of the staff had made their transition difficult. At Spring Haven, the CNAs who had been friendly toward Cora when she first helped her parents move in, now averted their gaze when she walked by them in the hallway. If a Spring Haven employee walked by her father without acknowledging him, her father would say loudly, "Christ, these people have shitty attitudes. Nobody should treat old people like this."

He began to answer her question.

"One of the helpers, Henry, took the laundry out this morning. He's the one who is in school full time and he only works here two days a week, you know?" He paused for her to acknowledge she knew Henry, so she responded with "Mm hmm," even though she couldn't place him.

"But he works long shifts and he's always tired. He came in to help with your mother, which he did half-assed, like they all do, and when he was leaving, I had to *ask* him to take the laundry with him, like I'm asking him for a goddamn favor. Like it's not his *job*." The familiar inflection of her father's voice when he said he *asked* the CNA to take the laundry caused her jaw to clench. "So, he grabbed the laundry basket and as he's leaving, he *banged* it against the door! I told him he needed to have *respect* for other people's property, and he just left without saying anything " Cora imagined Henry hurrying out of the room, trying to escape her father's harangue, a movement she'd perfected in childhood. "Another one of them—I don't know which one —it's hard to tell some of those women apart — brought the clean laundry back just a little while ago and I guess I should have gone through it right when she dropped it off, but I didn't realize I had to check on *every god damn thing they do*." His cadence slowed, and he stressed each of the last few words. "And when I went to put the laundry in the drawer just now, I noticed one of your mother's socks was missing."

Cora pulled a workout shirt from her dryer, folded it roughly, and added it to the growing pile of folded clothes on the counter. She looked over at the phone laying face up on the tile and took a deep breath and waited.

"For Christ's sake, how hard is it to keep two socks together in the laundry?" Cora hung back, not sure if he was finished talking. "I guess that's what you get when you pay people minimum wage and when no one in this place knows how to manage anything." With that sentence, the inevitable variation of 'no one anywhere knows how to do anything as well as I do', Cora knew he was finished, and she should respond.

"Dad," she said, trying to keep her voice upbeat and nonjudgmental. "I don't think it's a minimum wage issue or an incompetence issue. Socks get lost in the dryer all the time."

"What are you *talking* about?" He sputtered the words and Cora pictured the spit flying from his mouth. "Socks *don't just disappear.*" His certainty was absolute, and her thoughts flashed back to her dad's sock drawer in the antique wooden dresser he had when she was young. He kept his socks in the second drawer from the top, the dresser covered with a starched and pressed white dresser scarf which he laid his wallet and keys on each night when he returned home from work. She loved to follow him up to his room when he came home from work, standing in the doorway and watching as he emptied his pockets and then shooing her away so he could change out of his work clothes, his starched white shirts crumpled by the day's work, his dark suits in need of a little freshening. She used to sneak into his room when he wasn't home to inspect the contents of his dresser, intrigued by the photos of his parents, his folded and neatly ironed handkerchiefs lined up in a pile on the left-hand corner of the dresser, the yellowing photo of her mother as a teenager.

Cora would open his sock drawer, marveling at its organization, each pair of socks rolled up carefully, one sock folded over the other to make a tight, uniform roll, the rolls of socks lined up in perfect order in the small drawer lined with shelf paper. He'd learned to roll his socks in the army, he told Cora, and he had tried many times to get Cora and her mother to roll theirs in the same manner. His wife, who acquiesced to most of his demands, held firm against this one, for reasons that Cora never understood. She would, however, wash and dry his tidily paired, dirty socks in a mesh bag and deliver them to the chair next to his dresser. Her father would then roll them and neatly put them away.

Cora realized, as she stood looking at the hastily folded pile of laundry, it was quite likely that none of her father's socks had ever disappeared because of this washing method. In her experience as a wife and a mother, socks disappeared *all the time.* Her son never seemed to get both socks into the laundry hamper simultaneously, so there was rarely a laundry day where the number of socks that came out of the dryer was divisible by two. Her solution to this was twofold. She kept all the stray, unpaired socks in a sock basket on top of the dryer where her family could find socks when they needed. And at Christmas, she bought twelve-packs of white athletic socks from Costco and wrapped them up and put them under the Christmas tree.

"Dad, socks disappear in the dryer all the time. It's a thing. Google it." She tried to keep her tone light as she pulled one of the last two garments out of the dryer and slowly folded it.

"It's just *carelessness.* You put two socks into the dryer, two socks come out of the dryer. It's as simple as that."

It's *not* really carelessness, Cora wanted to argue. Maybe just a difference in priorities. But she knew enough not to interrupt him. "People need to learn to take care of their things, that's all. Nobody has *any* respect for *anything anymore.*" His voice had deflated, as though his rage had leaked out. "They hire people to work here who don't want to work here, who don't want to work hard at all, and then they don't train them, and this is what happens. No respect for anything."

"Dad, seriously," she began, her voice consciously

chipper and upbeat, "this is a real phenomenon. It happens to everyone and nobody can explain it. Dryers just eat socks." She put the last of the clothes she had folded onto the pile and stood looking at the phone on the counter.

"Well, I think they're trying to take advantage of me." His voice was thin. "They think I'm old. But I'm not too old to know what the hell they're doing, and I'm not going to take it. I'm going to get us out of here and find a better place."

Cora took a deep breath. She had known the conversation would end up here, with him needing to move, find something better. She picked up the phone from the counter, tapped the speaker function off, and put the phone to her ear as she walked into the living room.

"Dad, you've only been there two months," Cora said gently, trying to soothe him.

"You have no idea what it's like here, so don't you talk about how long I've been here," he snapped, the pressure building behind his words again. "I've been here quite long enough to know what it's like and that I want to leave."

"OK," Cora said, as she sat down on the couch, leaning forward, elbows on her knees. "If you really don't want to stay there, then let's figure out the next step." She hoped that offering this would stop his complaining.

"If we'd just stayed in our apartment, everything would

have been fine." Her dad stayed his course. "Christ, how did this happen?" He paused, but Cora knew he wasn't waiting for her to respond, so she kept quiet.

"One day, you're on top of the world. You have a good job, a nice family, a healthy nest egg for retirement. Then you retire, and you think it's going to be the life of your dreams, enjoying everything you worked so hard for." His voice trailed off. Cora listened to him breathe for a few seconds. She thought of her mother, who she knew was sitting in her chair positioned next to her husband's, the positions they had assumed throughout the nearly sixty years of their marriage. Night after night, they'd sat in those chairs, him watching TV with a book open on his lap, often dozing, her with an elaborate knitting project spread out, her dexterous fingers carrying out the system of hieroglyphic symbols that formed the elaborate patterns she followed. Her mother never watched the TV, treating it as background noise for her creativity. Sitting there had always seemed to Cora to be her mother's duty. Now, Cora knew, her parents sat together in their chairs, her father on the phone, the TV going in the background, her mother's gaze drawn to the flickering lights of the screen, her hands empty in her lap.

He continued. "But life's not like that at all. Even if you do everything right, it doesn't work out the way you think it's going to." He coughed softly. "It's not fair. None of this is goddamn fair."

Whoever said life was fair? Cora heard her father utter that phrase many times during her childhood when she'd complained about something not working out to her advantage. Now, Cora wanted to say this back to him, to point out that everyone got old and had bad things happen to them. But what she really wanted was for him to get up out of that chair and fight back. To grab her mother's hand and take her for a walk. Everyone lost a sock every now and then, Cora wanted to say, and life went on. But you had to get back up and live it.

Instead of pushing back, Cora stayed quiet and listened.

"Once my foot heals completely, I can take care of your mother again." Her father's tone was defiant, almost daring Cora to challenge his assertion. "So, I think you should look for a new apartment for us. Then it can just be me and your mother again, without all this other bullshit."

Just the mention of moving her parents back into an apartment caused Cora to slump back against the couch. In order to get through the last move from their apartment to the assisted living facility, she'd hired an organizer to help sort through her parents' things. Her father, his broken foot freshly casted after the surgery that had pinned his bones back together, sat in his chair and yelled at both Cora and the organizer when they asked him questions or suggested donating items they would no longer need or have room for. He'd wanted to take everything from their apartment and move it into the assisted living room, every book and record album, all the knickknacks and artwork collected from their travels. Compromising in any way enraged him.

"I'm not dead yet, goddamn it, and I'm not going to live like I am," he'd bellowed when Cora had suggested maybe not cramming so much into such a small space. In the end, Cora had filled her garage with her parents' belongings, promising her father that she'd keep the boxes safe and return them when her parents moved to a bigger place. Each day getting to her car, Cora walked by the artifacts of their life; the keyboard she'd given her father for Christmas twenty-five years earlier, complete with a stand and sheet music for Frank Sinatra's greatest hits, old family photographs, her parents' high school yearbooks, her grandmother's rosary beads and bible, newspaper clippings detailing engagements and weddings of friends nearly fifty years earlier.

"Dad," Cora said gently, "we need help taking care of mom. You know you can't take care of her on your own." Cora closed her eyes and listened to his ragged breathing. She desperately wanted this conversation to end. She didn't know what the answer should be to all of this. There didn't seem to *be* an answer.

"Do you know of any place we can go?" he asked, his voice startlingly small, his question shocking her eyes open. "Can you ask around and maybe get the names of some places we can go see?"

"I can talk to some people, Dad," Cora said haltingly. She knew she was lying. She didn't know who to ask for recommendation or what questions to ask. She didn't know what she was looking for.

Cora drew in a breath, preparing to utter the next sentence that she'd formulated in her mind. She knew speaking it out loud was a risk, but she pushed herself to say it without thinking of the consequences. "I'm not sure what you're looking for that you don't already have where you are." Her grip tightened around the phone, leg muscles tensed, ready to spring.

"I'm looking for people who *care!*" The anger was back, full force. "People who treat people with *respect!* You don't know what it's like here. You're not here." He took in a sharp, hitched breath. "They think they can do whatever they want to old people, and when I tell them they can't, they get mad. *They* get mad at *me!*" His voice was frantic. Cora needed to move away from the force of his voice. She stood up and walked quickly through the family room and into the kitchen. She walked in circles, swinging her arms out wide with the phone in her left hand, no longer listening, around the kitchen island, once, twice, three times, before putting the phone back up against her ear. "I'm not going to let them treat me like this," he said, unaware that she had disengaged. "And I'm sure as hell not leaving your mother here for them to treat *her* like that. Can you imagine what they'd do to her if I wasn't here?"

Cora stopped walking and leaned back against the shiny marble countertop. She didn't want to imagine how her mother was being cared for, or not cared for. Cora tried really hard, most of the time, not to think about what was happening to her mother at all. And her father had made that possible. Cora's mother had disappeared from her life years ago, bit by bit, without comment from either of her parents. Even before the dementia diagnosis, things had just shifted. Her father had taken over buying Christmas presents for her and the family, presents chosen from Amazon wish lists and internet links. Her father began taking mother away for holidays, or spending them alone, just the two of them in their apartment. "Your family can be too much for your mother," her father had said, explaining her withdrawal. And her mother had simply retreated from life, without a word of regret or farewell.

"I can't imagine, Dad," Cora said. "But what do you think about giving Spring Haven a few more weeks before you make a decision and see how you feel then?"

"Christ," he swore softly. And then he snapped, "How do you think I'm going to feel? How would you feel?"

"Bad, Dad. I'd feel bad." Cora wanted him to stop talking to her about this. She thought fleetingly of dinner tucked in the microwave, no longer spinning in the eerie light, growing cold and crusty around the edges. There was no way she could see to fix this situation with her parents, no way to make it better in any way. She wanted her father to take care of it, like he'd done with so many things before. She wanted him to have the answer for this. Because she didn't have one.

"Yes, you would." He went on. "This place isn't bad to *look* at, you know. They made it look nice and fancy and everything's new. There are big rooms with televisions and puzzles and pianos. As far as these kinds of places go, this one *looks* better than most of them. But it's the people. You just can't imagine the people. It's like they're all crazy!" Cora's dad coughed loudly into the phone, wheezing as he exhaled. "Every one of them has something wrong with them. I can't figure out how they got so many of them with things wrong, all in one place." His voice deflated. "I'm not a people person, and here, there's always someone around. It's like you're under a microscope. You go and eat with the same people every meal. They say the same things, sometimes word for word, every meal. They don't understand what's happening, and they ask the same questions, over and over." His voice trailed off and softened. "Some days, I just don't want to do it."

"I'm sorry, Dad," Cora said quietly, consciously pushing the panic she felt away from her vocal cords and back into her abdomen where it was already causing a sharp pain. "It sounds really tough." Cora pulled away from the countertop where she'd been leaning and took a few steps over to the microwave. She pulled the microwave door open and picked up the container of her dinner. She placed it on the counter and went back and shut the microwave with her free hand. "Maybe we can look around for another place for you. See if there's someplace you'll like better."

"Christ," he mumbled, his emotions spent. Cora stared at her dinner, no longer hungry.

"How about I bring mom some new socks when I come over on Sunday, just in case they never find the missing one." Cora forced a lightness into her tone.

"You'd better bring a few pair because if it happened once, it'll happen again. These people are morons."

Cora laughed softly. "Is there anything *you* need, Dad? Anything I can bring you?"

"Yeah, I need a new Porsche," her dad said, his voice tiny, a small wry laugh punctuating the end of his sentence.

Cora laughed again. "I'll get right on that, Dad. I'll have one ready to drive up on Sunday."

"Christ," he said faintly. "Wouldn't that be something'

"I'll see you Sunday, Dad." Cora paused. "Hang in there."

"See you Sunday," he said quietly, before he hung up.

Elizabeth Bobst

Elizabeth Bobst is a writer, editor, and educator focusing on ESOL and international education. Currently, she works with adults and families learning English as a second language. Interested in sharing culture as well as language, Elizabeth has taught in several different countries. Currently, Elizabeth lives and writes in North Carolina with her Irish Wolfhound, Lucy.

Silent Tears
By Sandra Brooks

What would have happened if I had acted that night instead of sitting frozen in the backseat of that Coupe de Ville while tears streamed silently down my face in the darkness? Would anything be different...would I, would they? That night was over 50 years ago and as I watch the horror of the racism in our country today, I realize the answer is no. And yet this event has haunted me since it happened one sultry, summer evening riding down a country road so long ago in the Mississippi Delta.

***

It was the summer of 1966 and I had just finished my freshman year in college. My dad helped me get a job working at the county campaign office for the favored gubernatorial candidate because he knew the campaign manager, Mr. Charlie Johnson. I was excited to be able to make extra spending money. My parents could only afford to send me to the local two-year community college, but luckily I was awarded a scholarship to a university two hours away from my hometown. We were a lower middle-class family with little left after bills were paid. Although we didn't have money, everyone loved my dad and he loved everybody. He was friends with the janitor at our church as well as the mayor of our small Southern town and even Mr. Charlie, who was the wealthiest man in the county. Friendship lines were more defined for us kids. My friends came from families similar to ours in economic status, but occasionally I would be invited to a party hosted by the popular, wealthier girls if they were inviting most of the class. Like many towns in the deep South back then, everyone was pretty status conscious, and you could only be accepted into the inner circle if your Daddy made enough money to afford a house in the "right" part of town and you could dress the part.

***

Of course, I am only speaking of the white people because schools were still segregated at that time and blacks lived in separate neighborhoods. I remember questioning my parents about why we didn't all go to school together and why blacks couldn't eat in the same restaurants and why they didn't attend our churches and on and on. They usually told me that black people preferred their own schools and churches and they liked different foods, or sometimes the answer was simply, "It's just always been that way." I wasn't really satisfied with their answers, but I grew up being taught that children respect adults and don't question. We were literally taught to be "seen and not heard". "Why" questions were not welcome from anyone who was still dependent on their parents. I remember one time when I was about thirteen and was persistently questioning my mother about racial issues. Finally, as punishment she made me go to my room with no dinner for being disrespectful. Interestingly, I didn't think of my parents as racists because I never heard them use derogatory language about or toward black people and hadn't witnessed either of them overtly treating a person differently because of skin color. Segregation and racial bias never made sense to me and I was pretty obsessed with the subject, but growing up during that time in that place, distorts your perception and ability to see or even think clearly about the injustices around you. I was naïve, sheltered and ignorant of much outside of my narrow, little Southern existence. But I couldn't fight the feeling that I had been born in the wrong place or at the wrong time.

***

Mr. Charlie called to say the campaign office was opening on Monday and he would meet me there for orientation and to go over my daily responsibilities. He introduced me to Mr. Ed Hightower, his assistant campaign manager, who would be my primary contact for questions. I had heard colorful stories about Mr. Charlie and his wife,

Mrs. Dorothy, from my dad. They were in their early 60's, were known for elaborate parties at their mansion on the hill and were prominent pillars of the community. When I was in high school, I worked at the corner drugstore after school three days a week and during summers. Mrs. Dorothy came in one day and asked me to help her find lipstick to match her new candy apple red Cadillac that Mr. Charlie had just given her. He had also purchased a white matching sedan for himself. She said he always bought both of them a new Cadillac every two years, but this was her first red one. I remember being in awe of such wealth and privilege. I imagined that this must be the way Hollywood stars live. I knew Mr. Charlie owned a ranch and showed Tennessee walking horses and I never asked how he got to be so wealthy. The love of horses was the common denominator between him and my dad. Although my dad had a passion for quarter horses, he had a reputation for knowing more about horses that almost anyone in the area and that commanded Mr. Charlie's respect. So there I was in June of 1966 at the age of 18 working for this local powerful man and he was telling me that part of my job would include going with him and Mrs. Dorothy to political rallies around the state. I was feeling pretty fortunate and looking forward to my summer.

***

There was rarely anyone else working in the office with me and I loved the independence. I spent my days answering phone calls, handing out bumper stickers and campaign buttons to visitors who stopped by, stuffing envelopes, and preparing materials for the next rally. Mr. Charlie and Mrs. Dorothy were so gracious and invited me to their home for dinner several times where I met senior members of the campaign from the state headquarters. Many times after dinner when the political work discussions were winding down, I would go into the kitchen to chat with the maid while the rest of the adult group migrated into the living room with their cocktails. Her name was Jesse and I loved our conversations. She told me about her family and how much she wanted to go to Chicago to visit her sister. Her dream for both daughters and her son was for them to get a college education. She told me that maybe she should just be grateful if they could graduate from high school and get jobs. You could feel her love and pride as she talked about her children. She had one of the kindest faces I had ever seen. Jesse had worked for the Johnsons over 10 years and she said they were very good to her. We developed a special bond during those long conversations and agreed we shared good bosses in Mr. Charlie and Mrs. Dorothy. They made me feel like a valued member of the team, but I wasn't sure it was the same for

Jesse. After all, she wasn't invited to sit down with us for dinner which I couldn't understand. We had never had a maid and neither had anyone I knew other than the Johnsons, so I didn't have much of a reference point.

***

It was the first week in August and my last week working for the campaign. Our candidate was leading in the polls and almost certain to be the new governor. I was feeling excited as I prepared all of the promotional materials for the night's rally which would be my last. The work had been fun and I learned a lot about the internal complexities of political campaigns. In addition, I had saved enough to buy new clothes for next semester. I drove to the Johnsons for the last time, loaded all of the posters, buttons, brochures, etc. into the trunk of Mr. Charlie's Cadillac and climbed into the back seat with Mrs. Dorothy. Mr. Hightower was in the front seat with Mr. Charlie as was the customary seating arrangement. The rally was about three hours away, so Jesse had packed a cooler with drinks and lots of yummy homemade snacks. Jesse had already gone for the day when I arrived, so I didn't get to say goodbye to her. I wanted to hug her and tell her how much I had grown to love her, but that never happened. I didn't realize this would be the last time I would ever see Mr. Charlie and Mrs. Dorothy.

***

We spent much of the travel time to the rally laughing and talking about various events of the summer surrounding the campaign. Jesse's delicious snacks were consumed by the four of us with many comments from the Johnsons about what a loyal, dependable maid she was. The three-hour drive passed quickly as we drove through the Delta with cotton fields on each side of the road. Mr. Charlie was especially jovial because he had worked hard to get his candidate elected plus had donated thousands to his campaign. As we approached the fairgrounds where the rally was being held, we could see there was a record crowd. Mr. Charlie found someone to unload the collateral material and we four headed to the main tent to meet up with the key speakers including the winning candidate who was obviously overjoyed with the prospects of being elected. It was the best rally of the summer.

***

Still drawing from the enthusiasm of the crowd although it was getting late, we headed back home. The men lit cigars and I remember Mr. Charlie saying with a huge belly laugh, "Damn, Ed, I think we've got this one in the bag!" I had just looked over the seat at the clock on the dashboard and the time was 10:30. We were about an hour and a half from home when it happened. The men were still feeling energized and were telling stories about growing up in Mississippi. Most of the tales were funny and innocuous. Mrs. Dorothy was dozing in the backseat because I'm sure she had heard most of the stories before and was getting tired. I was wide awake and enjoying the two older gentlemen having such a good time reminiscing although I was totally quiet and they probably thought I had fallen asleep too. Then, Mr. Charlie asked Ed if he had ever told him about the time he and his brother had discovered that a 16-year-old boy on their plantation had stolen a radio from the guest house. Ed said, "No, man, I don't think I've heard that one." Mr. Charlie chuckled and began to relate the story. I had no warning that something was about to shift inside me and I would never be the same. He said his dad was pretty upset about the radio but decided not to make a big deal of it because James' family were great workers and it was just one mistake. Mr. Charlie and his brother, David, who were both home for the summer had always thought James was a little "uppity" black kid and decided to take matters into their own hands. James was walking back to his family's shack one night about dusk when Mr. Charlie, 19, and David, 17, ran out of the bushes and chased him into the cotton fields. My heart was racing as I started to realize this story was not like the rest. Mr. Charlie continued, "We caught him about 200 yards between the cotton rows and threw him down in the dirt. He was begging us not to hurt him. We had already determined we were not just going to teach him a lesson. It was pretty dark, but I could still see the whites of his eyes and smell his fear. I had brought my deer knife and we sliced him open." James commented that he probably wouldn't be listening to any music on the radio now….uppity N…. "Yeah, I always thought he was worthless. We had hidden a saw in the bushes, so we stuffed all of the pieces into a cotton sack." I realized tears were pouring down my face and I had been holding my breath. I couldn't think; my head was spinning; I was totally nauseous. What do I do? Somehow I realized in that moment that as an 13 year-old in this situation, I could not do or say anything. All my programming came flooding into my mind at once….be respectful, he seen but not heard, never confront an adult, don't ask questions, be quiet. I don't know if it was my survival instincts, immobilizing fear or just pure cowardice that took over. I still can't adequately describe that moment after all of these years. I think I left my body so I couldn't feel anything because I have no memory of anything the rest of the night, even driving myself home. I didn't hear anything that was said after "stuffed all the pieces into the cotton sack". I suppose I said goodbye to the Johnsons, but I'm not sure. All I know was I was consumed with guilt, shame, deep sadness and horror. I had just heard the accounting of a murder and felt like I had personally witnessed it....and I DID NOTHING. I walked around in some sort of altered state before going back to college. I never said a word to my parents about that night and although they were concerned about my behavior, they decided it was just anxiety about going back to school. Two weeks passed before I completely fell apart. I left classes crying uncontrollably. I thought about Jesse and wanted to talk to her, but I didn't know how to call her and what would I even say to her. I woke up soaked in sweat from nightmares about bloody

cotton sacks. In one nightmare Mr. Charlie was laughing at me and saying, "Damn, I think we've got this one in the bag."

***

And here we are in 2020 and George Floyd has been murdered. The tears are still streaming down my face, but I have not been silent since that summer in 1966.

Sandra Brooks

Sandra Brooks has reinvented herself several times from entrepreneur, jewelry designer, life coach, realtor and always a seeker of truth and equality for all. Having lived in the South much of her life, she loves the richness of its culture but also strives to expose the deep injustices that continue to lurk in the shadows of its mighty oaks.

Her love of travel introduced her to a world of people, cuisines, customs and languages inviting her to embrace diversity and find joy in the differences as much as the similarities. Sandra's writing often reflects experiences gained through her explorations around the world as well as her years as a Southern girl growing up in the Deep South. She worked over 20 years in Manhattan and always felt as much at home strolling the streets of New York as she did picking beans in the family garden back in Mississippi.

Writing is her way of sharing herself and her gratitude for all of life… the good and the bad.

Fun, Fun, Fun with Dick and Jane
By Wayne Fowler

For the briefest time, only one day as a matter of fact, young Ohmie and the girl shared a few precocious hours in a day care facility. Ohmie's parents, anxious to advance their son's education, as well as to afford themselves a few hours respite each day, enrolled him in day care. They were asked not to bring him back after the first day; the girl lasted out the week. Neither Ohmie, nor the girl, held memories of the ordeal. Neither set of parents knew any other child's identity.

The day began ordinarily enough: a story, lessons, playtime, a snack, more stories and lessons, naptime, and etcetera through the day.

"'Look up, Dick said,'" the teacher read from a popular story book.

"'Look up, up, up.'"

"How high up?" Ohmie asked, injecting his question between the teacher's breaths. Her mouth smiled; her eyes did not smile. "Past the stratosphere? Into the troposphere? Or just as far as ol' cumulus nimbus?"

The girl laughed. She was the only one who did. The teacher certainly did not laugh. She did not laugh at all.

She looked cross and did not laugh.

Ohmie looked at her expectantly, though content to listen for enlightenment further into the tale.

The teacher continued after a whole-body sigh, "'Jane said, run, run. Run, Dick, run. Run and see.'" The teacher glanced through her eyebrow at Ohmie, keeping a wary eye on him.

Seeing an opportunity, and following Ohmie's lead, the girl asked, "What's he running from? Or to? And what is there to see?"

The teacher's face reddened but she smiled grimly as she instructed the girl to just wait and see for herself.

Ohmie smiled at the girl, noticing her for the first time. Her light brown hair was in a ponytail. Her missing front teeth gave her a younger appearance which belied her precocious nature.

"'Look, look, said Dick.'" The teacher continued reading, quickly, more quickly than ordinarily, jumping to the next line when she might otherwise take a breath and look up to smile at each child. Routinely, she would allow children time to absorb the words and thoughts. On this occasion her focus was on closing the gap, eliminating any opening for interruption, especially for Ohmie. She did not ever like to be questioned about a story. She did not like it at all. She always had trouble relocating her place in the book.

She was beginning to not like Ohmie very much, or the girl that she felt Ohmie had influenced, though she truly wanted to.

"'See Sally. See funny Sally and Father.'" At this point the teacher was compelled to turn the book toward the children since the story more or less directed the readers (and listeners) to see the book's illustration, a picture of Father walking toward Dick and Jane with little Sally on his shoulder, she wearing his fedora.

"Is that a fedora?" Ohmie asked a decibel above the other children's oohing and ahhing. "I haven't seen one of those in years, maybe never. Is it made of felt?"

The girl snickered, alternating glances from Ohmie to the teacher.

Ohmie contented himself to not be answered.

The teacher pretended that she had not heard Ohmie at all.

The teacher read the next lines, hopeful that ignoring Ohmie would teach him silence and proper decorum. "'See, see', said Sally. Sally is up, up, up. This is fun for Sally.'"

"Maybe for Sally, but she's wearin' me out, out, out," Ohmie said under his breath, heard only by the girl who'd inched her way toward him while the others inched toward the teacher and her book. Ohmie did not like to pronounce the 'g' at the end of 'ing' words. He thought they were unnecessary. And highfalutin.

At recess the two new friends mimed and mimicked the Dick and Jane story.

"Look, look," Ohmie said. "Look up to the demonstrations of spectral phenomenon: the gnats at head height, robins, robins and sparrows above them, up, up, up, to the mourning doves and starlings. Look up, up, up and see, see, see the hawks and vultures far above the canopy. Look through, through, through, through the cirrus cumulus to the contrails left by the commercial airliners, the sevens: 707 through 787, not to mention Boeing's one thousand series. Look up, Jane, look up, up, up at the evidence of economic prowess."

The girl did not look up any higher than the two inches Ohmie stood taller than herself. "Yer gonna get into big trouble," she cautioned, but she really did not want him to stop his cleverness. "I can feel, feel feel it coming."

Ohmie grinned widely.

Mind-numbing repetitions of numbers, letters, shapes and colors just about blinded Ohmie during lesson time after recess. The girl commiserated, sending mellowing vibrations of empathy his way.

The announcement of another *Dick and Jane* story almost made Ohmie barf, barf, barf. A library full of books, and... Ohmie was certain she selected the additional Dick and Jane story to punish, punish, punish him.

"'Dick said, Who is here?'" the teacher read. "'Who is it, Mother?'"

The teacher showed her class the picture of Dick standing behind his seated mother, his hands over her eyes. The class shouted out in near unison, "It's Dick!"

Ohmie and the girl rolled their eyes in unison.

The teacher continued, "'Oh, Mother, said Dick. You can see who it is.'" Once again, the teacher showed her class the accompanying picture.

"There's Father!" shouted one of the children, followed by a cacophony about the dog and other pictorially depicted drivel.

"It's a Britty Spaniel!" shouted a large child.

"Brittany Spaniel," corrected the teacher.

A waiting Ohmie seized the opportunity by the horns. "It's actually an English Springer Spaniel. They rank 13th on the Stanley Coren's dog intelligence list. Brittanies are only 18th. English Springer's are better for families with more than one kid 'cause Brittanies often bond with a single individual, but you have to watch for the rage syndrome. That's why you need to get one from a field-bred line, not a show-dog line."

Ohmie had learned from the teacher not to offer gaps

wide enough for insertions. The girl noted that Ohmie toyed with the teacher with his rapid-fire oration. The instant the teacher's lips began to form a word, Ohmie kicked his homily into high gear, raising the pitch just slightly.

"See, rage syndrome is when a dog goes glassy-eyed and then attacks. It usually only lasts a few seconds. It's like the dog forgets it's tame. There's a study that red-haired spaniels are meanest. Do you think there's a human correlation? Anybody? Anybody?" he asked, catching the teacher off guard. Taking advantage of her obvious consternation, Ohmie quickly appropriated her opportunity. "You can't be leavin' spaniels alone, though. That's when they go to barkin' an' tearin' stuff up, up, up."

The girl burst out laughing but tried very hard to hide it behind her hand.

The teacher, beyond knowing how to deal with Ohmie, directed a rancor toward the girl's outburst. "Now children, we mustn't encourage... disruptive... disorderly...

"Now. Where were we," the teacher asked in an effort to return the class to order. She shouldn't have asked, she told herself a second later.

"About to see how dumb, dumb, dumb Mom is when she doesn't recognize Dad's hairy hands over her eyes, or his gravelly voice." In a sudden and furious diatribe of recitation, Ohmie cited the book's next page lines, lines he'd memorized when the teacher last displayed the previous page's picture.

"'Who is this? said Father,'" Ohmie quoted, reciting the rest of the page in a bat's blink. "'Who is it? Mother said, It is not Dick. It is not Jane. It is not little Baby Sally. It is big, big Father. Yes, yes, said Baby Sally. Oh, Mother, you can see.'"

Ohmie crossed his arms over his chest, smiling, and glared at the teacher. The girl crossed her arms and glared at Ohmie, nodding at the culmination of her wise prediction that he would get into trouble. All the other children sat in silence at the teacher's glowing hue. Her right eye was twitching.

"Nap time!" she fairly shouted as she tossed the book across her desk, sending it flying to the floor after its touch-n-go non-landing.

The teacher didn't notice the girl's gravitation to Ohmie's side, edging her nap rug beside his. All her attention on the intractable Ohmie.

Instinctively the two understood that their communication would have to be surreptitious. Mind-reading between them seemed more natural than words, each understanding full meanings of the slightest expression.

Up, up, up, Ohmie expressed with his head and eyes.

Down, down, down, the girl returned as she closed her eyes in an effort to discern Ohmie's subconscious brainwaves.

Finding her thoughts calmed him, turning his own thoughts from up, up, up to her, her, her.

The teacher used nap time to call Ohmie's parents, requesting they come and get him immediately. She would need to have a serious talk, talk, talk with them.

The End

Wayne Fowler

Wayne Fowler wasn't expected to live, not by anyone who knows him. Upon introduction and acquaintance, his antics are at poisonous opposition to his benign character. None predicted more than six months. Who knew that he had already lived many millennium in the guise of Ohmie, a precocious gambol, springing up un-heralded age after age.

Wayne was a U. S. Marine (1968-1972), a mailman, among other things (USPS 1973-2006), and a businessman (2001-2019). Now he ain't nothin' but a happy traveler.

Wayne lives in Arkansas with his wife, Debbie. He can be followed, after a fashion, on Facebook, and in Wayne and Debbie's blog at: themirthfulroadrunners.tumblr.com/

Fins Fatal Flop
By Kaye George

Fin thought the new girl was gonna be okay. Some of them worked out, some didn't. They usually came to The Flirty Flamingo from bad places– drugs, prostitution, abuse. Mostly they were runaways. He couldn't picture the new one, Charn, running, but she sure was trying to escape something.

Looking at her now, sitting at the other end of the bar sipping a ginger ale, waiting to go on stage, he saw how smooth her pretty face was, how relaxed her small, thin body sat.

When she came in the door two weeks ago, her face was scrunched in fear. She held her shoulders high and tight, folding in on herself to try to make herself invisible, even smaller.

"Hey, sweetie." Fin was beside her in a flash. He didn't miss much of what went on in the bar. "You need some help?"

She cringed and shrank away from him, but he kept talking, soft and calm. "You're okay here. We'll take care of you. You need a place to stay for awhile?"

She nodded, tears beginning to flow over her young, softly curved cheeks.

"Follow me." He avoided touching her. The kid has been hurt and didn't need to be spooked when she was so close to finding a hiding place.

She trailed behind him to the back office where Joe, the bartender, kept the books and stored some of the more expensive liquors. Fin unlocked the door and stood aside. Giving him a questioning look, she hesitated, then crossed the threshold and stepped into the small room.

It took some time, but Fin eventually learned that her name was Charn Jones. Maybe a real name, maybe not, but it's what she told him. She'd left home a year ago to try to make it as a singer. She hadn't gotten far before she picked up an admirer.

"I thought he liked me," she said, her voice low, looking at her feet as she sat in Joe's big leather chair, rubbing the smooth, worn armrests. "But he started being mean to me. Then he wouldn't let me go anywhere. When I got to go out sometimes, he'd follow me, not let me talk to anyone."

"Do you have any family?" Sometimes, Fin knew, these girls had families that were worried about them. Sometimes they didn't.

"My mother's boyfriend left. She got a new one. She thought he liked me better than her, so she told me to get out."

So, she didn't have a family worth the name.

"You hungry, kid?"

She nodded. Finn told her to wait in the office and he went to find Alice. Alice didn't go on stage anymore. She worked the bar part time and filled in where she could. Alice rustled up a couple of sandwiches and a Coke and brought them to the office.

"Here you go, honey," Alice said. "You look hungry."

Charn looked up at Alice and almost smiled. "I am." She took a half a sandwich with the tips of her fingers. "Thank you, miss."

Alice leaned down, a considerably distance since Alice was so tall and thin, wiry and tough. To Fin, she was perfect. His gaze usually softened when he looked at Alice. She'd been with him for a few years, both of them kicking around the bar, Fin providing security and odd jobs, Alice tending bar part time. She hadn't been on the stage in a long time.

"You take your time," Alice said to Charn. "Eat as much as you want. No one's gonna rush you." Alice straightened up. "If you want to talk to me, my name's Alice. I'm a good listener."

Alice and Fin had that talent in common, that ability to listen, to *really* listen to a person. Fin's mother had wanted him to be a priest. Instead, he wound up listening to confessions in a stripper joint.

On her way out the door, Alice looked at Fin. "Phineas—" she was the only person in the world who call him Phineas "—have her come see me later. I'll get her some clothes."

After Charn looked a little less like she might drop from hunger, Fin ushered her up the back stairs and showed her to a room with a bed and clean linens, bath next door. "Get some sleep, kid. We'll talk later."

Charn stayed, became one of them. After about a week, she worked up an act. She had a golden voice and strummed a mean guitar. Joe had a couple three of them stashed somewhere, left behind by other performers. Most of the girls at the Flamingo did either pole dances or stripteases, or a combo, but Charn, who should have been named Charm, because she did that—charmed the drinkers into throwing money at her without taking her clothes off. Her sweet voice and her innocent, clear blue eyes tore the bills right out of their hands and the bills flew onto the stage. Alice had sewed Charn an outfit to accentuate her best qualities and go with her personality, pink and ruffly and feminine, a little risqué, with feathers in strategic places, like all the Flamingo costumes for the other girls.

Fin moved to the seat next to Charn. She didn't shy

away or flinch. She even looked at him and smiled. Progress, he thought.

"How's it going?" he asked. "You've been here two weeks. You think you want to stay?"

Alice was helping Joe behind the bar and she lingered, listening to the conversation.

Charn looked at both of them. "Yes, if I can. Do you think I can? Am I bringing in enough money?"

Alice patted her hand, resting on the counter beside her sweating glass of ginger ale. "This place does all right. Don't worry about it. If you need to stay, you can."

A slight frown wrinkled Charn's brow. "I don't know that I need to, but I want to. Is that okay?"

"It is, darlin," Alice assured her. Alice moved on to take a couple of orders at the middle of the bar where two men had just come in. Not regulars, Fin noticed. New guys. One was small, skinny, young and pimply. The other one had some heft on him, a big burly guy that Fin might have a hard time taking down if he needed to. They had come in a few minutes apart and sat with two stools between them. Not together, obviously.

Fin was at the wrong end of the bar. At the other end, he could see the door and the whole room, so he wished Charn luck and rose to move back to his customary spot.

"Mr. Fin?" Charn looked a little worried. "Can I talk to

you later?"

"Sure thing, kiddo. Catch me after your set." After he sat, he watched Charn eyeing the two new guys at the middle of the bar. His attention sharpened. That was fear on the young woman's face. He kept his eyes on the men while Charn performed. They both left after her set, after a trip back to the loo for the bigger guy, then out the front door.

Fin talked to her later and she said she thought she saw someone she knew, but she was mistaken.

"You sure?" Fin remembered how they had both looked at her. Men who looked at the girls like that were sometimes trouble. They were both fixated on Charn.

"Yeah, it's fine. No problem."

The next night, Charn was off. The two men came back, this time within half an hour of each other. They each had a beer, then soon left. The following night, though, she was on again. This time, just one of them came in. He sat at the bar, following every move she made. He was the big, strong-looking guy. Long greasy dark hair and a stubble on his face that had gone too many days to look good.

He had hit the head before she went on and went back there again after she was done. When he came back, Fin followed him when he went out the front door. He gave the guy a few minutes lead time, then hit the sidewalk. The guy wasn't in sight. Fin strolled to the narrow alleyway between The Flirty Flamingo and the pawn shop next door. Sure enough, the guy was loitering at the side door. It was used for deliveries and kept locked most of the time. Maybe he thought Charn would go out that way, but she was still living upstairs, above the bar.

Fin eased his back against the bricks at the end of the alley and bided his time. Eventually, the guy left. He came back almost every night for a week, but quit going to the alley after Charn's show.

One night, after closing, Fin was in the office helping Joe count the take. Alice came in with a scowl on her face

"We got another Peeping Tom," she said.

The set up of the building had a flaw that would be too expensive to change. The public restroom was next to the dressing room the gals used, just off the stage. Periodically, a pervy customer realized it and took the time to carve a peephole in the wall.

"Damn," Joe said, standing up and pushing back his chair, banging it on the file cabinet behind him. "I gotta fix another goddam hole."

"Wait," Fin said. "Let me try to catch the perv. I been keepin an eye on a guy and I want to see if it's him or not He should be in tomorrow."

"That the guy looks like he's mooning over Charn?" Joe

asked.

"She says the guy she was worried about has stopped coming in," Alice said. "Charn's been telling me some things. She says she was turning tricks for a young, skinny guy. He was mistreating her and she got away, came here straight from him. She thought he'd been coming in here. But she decided his hair is wrong, she said. Her guy had red hair, kind of long. The one that came in has a blond buzz. He came in the same nights as a tough looking palooka a couple of times.

"Yeah, he stopped coming in. Palooka's been back, though," Fin said. "He was here tonight. I'll check him tomorrow night and see if he's the perv."

"I checked up on both the new guys," Alice continued. "The skinny one's done time. Aggravated assault. Name's Janis. Greg Janis. The other one, big guy, no record, if he's using his real name."

"What's he using?" Fin asked.

"Get this. Lacey Jones."

"I can't comment on people's names," Fin said. His full name was Phineas Pudlow.

Joe chuckled. "I guess not. So, the new guys are Janis and Lacey."

The Peeping Toms they'd had were never violent, but Fin considered what they did an assault on the girls. It was something done against their will, something personal. And creepy. But just because they'd never had to get physical with a peeper, didn't mean they never would. Fin gave some thought to this one. He needed a plan.

When they had finished counting the take for the night, Fin had made up his mind about the big guy. "Joe," he said. "If I have to tackle this guy, I'll need some help. Big Lacey outweighs me by quite a bit."

Fin wasn't big and didn't look tough, but knew how to move. He could hold his own in a lot of situations, but this might not be one of them.

"Sure," Joe said. "I'll put Alice on the bar and come back with you." Joe was medium sized, too, but had once trained in the ring. Being black, he'd thought at one time that boxing would be his ticket to the good life. It didn't take many punches for him to change his mind and switch gears. He worked his way up from washing dishes to bussing tables to serving to tending bar. Eventually, he was able to buy the one they all worked in now. But boxing had taught him a few things. He hadn't forgotten them.

"You better bring Bertha," Alice said. Alice always referred to Fin's Glock, the firearm from his days on the police force, as Bertha. Fin didn't usually carry it, but it came in handy sometimes, when someone needed convincing. People tended to be convinced by Bertha.

"And I'll bring her friend." Joe grinned. He always kept a .44 Magnum under the bar. In that neighborhood it wouldn't be smart not to. Alice called that one "Dirty Harry," but no one else ever referred to it that way.

The next night the skinny blond guy, Greg Janis, came in within minutes of the big mug. They both watched every move Charn made during her set. At the end of each number, when most of the mesmerized drinkers burst into applause and some even cheered, those two both sat stone-faced.

Sure enough, Palooka, aka Big Lacey, got up when Charn left the stage and headed for the bathroom. Fin was already sitting at the far end of the bar, next to the door that led to the hallway. He waited a half a beat before he pushed into the john. Big guy was in the stall.

"Open it up," Fin said, rapping on the door.

"What the hell? I'm busy in here."

Fin pulled a screwdriver out of his pocket, slipped it into the notch and unlatched the door. Lacey Jones was crouched, not on the toilet seat, but at the hole in the wall. He straightened up and started throwing angry punches in the confined space, hitting his knuckles on the metal side wall.

Fin backed out of the stall, ducking, and drawing the guy forward.

Joe had come in behind them. He stepped up beside Fin and trained his revolver on the perv. "Get outta my bar, and don't ever come back," Joe snarled.

Lacey's anger left his face and his big body deflated. "I didn't mean nothin. I'll go."

Just as I assumed, Fin thought. The peeper isn't really physically violent, just a disgusting pervert.

Fin and Joe heard the screams before the guy got through the door. They shoved him aside and raced to the dressing room.

When Fin threw the door open, two half-dressed strippers were cowering in the corner, screaming, while the skinny, blond guy held Charn by her throat, choking the life out of her.

Fin and Joe wrestled him off her and to the ground. Joe pulled a pair of zip ties from his pocket and bound the guy's wrists.

"That's him," Charn sobbed, her voice hoarse from the choking. "It really is him. I didn't think it was."

"Greg Janis? Was this the guy?" Fin asked.

"He told me he was Jay. That's the only name I knew for him," Charn croaked.

Fin whipped out his phone to summon the cops while Joe stood the skinny guy up.

Before Fin could finish the three numbers, he was hit

from behind. His phone flew out of his hand. He fell to the floor, blood gushing from his scalp. He tried to turn over. A heavy foot planted itself on his back.

Joe let go of the skinny guy, reached for his revolver, now tucked into his waistband.

"I wouldn't do that." Fin recognized the voice of the peeper. He struggled to turn his head enough to see a Smith & Wesson semi-automatic .45 being pointed at Joe with a shaky hand. "She's mine. I been lookin at her all these nights. She's mine, not yours. Shove her over here."

Joe focused somewhere behind the Palooka. Nodded. Threw skinny Janis to the floor and followed him down.

At almost the same instant, Fin heard the shot, felt the weight leave his back. Big Lacey Jones crashed, hard, to the floor. He bounced slightly, then lay still.

Fin raised himself on one elbow. Alice stood in the doorway with Bertha in her steady hand, pointed at the dead guy on the floor.

"I'll call the cops," Joe said, shoving little Janis into a chair, his hands zip tied uncomfortably behind him.

Fin got up and went to Alice, standing in a wide-eyed daze, still pointing the gun at Lacey. He gently took his Glock from her hands, laid it on a dressing table, and put his arms around her.

Alice held up well all the while she talked to the police.

They weren't inclined to take her in since her story was backed up by everyone else's, including Greg Janis. Charn retreated upstairs as soon as she'd been questioned. She said she didn't want any company, just needed to be alone that night.

After the cops left, their people taking the body and Charn's attacker with them, Alice started trembling violently.

"Who knew," she said through chattering teeth, "who knew that it wasn't the felon, it was the other guy we really had to watch out for?"

"You saved my life, sweetie," Fin said.

"Mine too." Joe was shaky himself. "I thought the plan was for you to take your gun with you tonight, Fin."

"I guess it was. At the last minute, I thought I wouldn't need it. Lacey Jones didn't have any history of violence. He was a peeper, for godsake. The other guy was the ex-con."

"They were b-b-both dangerous," Alice said, trembling in Fin's arms as they sat in a booth in the empty bar. "You couldn't have p-p-planned for that."

"We sure could have. You could have taken your damn gun with you, Fin," Joe growled. "We had a plan."

Fin nodded. "Yeah, we did. My bad." He gave Alice a fond look and a smile as her head rested on his shoulder. Inside, though, he ached. He knew what the weight of taking a life was like. Knew how it felt heavy on your shoulders, your heart, your soul. He caressed Alice's thin shoulders and vowed to help her support the weight.

"You gonna give Alice a raise, Joe?" he asked.

Joe grinned at both of them. "That sounds like a good plan."   THE END

Kaye George

Kaye George is the author of: People of the Wind pre-history mysteries, published by Untreed Reads, the first nominated for an Agatha Award for Best Historical Novel; two traditional series: Cressa Carraway musical mysteries, the first a finalist for the Silver Falchion Award; and the humorous Texas Imogene Duckworthy series, the first nominated for an Agatha for Best First Novel. Cozies: the Fat Cat series (all Barnes & Noble best-sellers) for Penguin (written as Janet Cantrell) and the latest: Vintage Sweets series from Lyrical Press.

More than fifty of her short stories have appeared online, in anthologies, magazines, her own collection, one thrillogy (Wildside Press), and her own anthology of eclipse stories, DAY OF THE DARK, also by Wildside Press. "Handbaskets, Drawers, and a Killer Cold," nominated for an Agatha for Best Short Story; Austin Mystery Writers' MURDER ON WHEELS, Silver Falchion Award winner; and recently "Dream Girl" placed second in the BOULD anthology of January 2019.

She is a member of Sisters in Crime, Guppies, Authors Guild of TN, Austin Mystery Writers, and lives in Knoxville, TN where she is the co-founder of Smoking Guns, the local Sisters in Crime chapter. She also reviews for Suspense Magazine.

Deluxe Accom
By Jim Gish

It was going to be an end of the year party. My dorm mates and I had finals in two weeks, and it was Stan who found out about the motel from a fellow Brooklynite who lived over in Faber Hall.

"The windows are all Xed out, and the TVA is going to flood the area. It officially belongs to the government, but this old fart still rents some of the rooms out by the night. We could get all the chickees and a bunch of booze and blast ourselves into an alcoholic coma!"

We laughed and high fived, and then we all gave Stan twenty bucks a piece which he put into an envelope. That was Thursday night. I called Heather, a girl I had dated off and on my sophomore year, and she said it sounded like fun. I had slept with her once or twice, and I knew she loved Jack and Coke.

It would be a good story for the boys back home that summer when I worked the burley patches and the hay fields. They always wanted "wild college girl" stories, and I always came through for them, although most of them were outright fiction or something that happened to somebody other than me. They didn't care.

When we got to the motel, there was still part of a sign,

and there was even a little neon circulating. Purple letters which spelled "Deluxe Accom" which must have once been Deluxe Accommodations, but that was in better years. When the four cars pulled in, and everyone got out, the owner came out in a ribbed undershirt, smoking a cigar and carrying a tall can of Pabst Blue Ribbon.

"You got the money, ain't you?" he said, burping out a shaft of beer breath.

Stan handed him the envelope, and he made a big deal out of counting each bill, like he thought we were going to cheat him because we were college kids.

When he was satisfied with the money, the little fat guy reached down to move his equipment around with his hand. This caused my girlfriend Heather to laugh out loud, and the cigar man turned toward her and gave her a gross kind of leer, like he thought maybe Heather was admiring his style.

"You ain't a bunch of fuckin' hippy Communists, are you?" he asked, giving the whole group one hard look.

"I ain't no fuckin hippy Communist, you old jerk off!" Stan said loudly, and spit once in the dirt.

"I been in the navy four years."

The old guy ignored the insult, and he shook Stan's hand and they said some Navy stuff to each other. About squadrons and admirals and carriers and shit we had no idea about.

Out of nowhere, I heard myself speaking to the man.

"I was born in Henderson County, sir," I told him. "I been workin' in burley tobacco since I was six years old."

The guy in the undershirt turned toward me and looked me in the eyes.

"Let me see them hands, boy," he said.

I walked over and held them out.

"Damn if you ain't , son," he said a little giddily. "Damn if you ain't a farm boy. Look at them callouses."

I had never been proud of my callouses before, but now my friend Bobby and the Brooklyn boys were looking at me with something like pride. Everybody had a nickname in the crowd, and I was named "Bobo" for no particular reason.

"Fuckin' Bobo, he's a straight on hick," Epstein said among the others and they laughed.

But the owner was finished with us. He tossed the keys to Stan and we drove to the back of the L shaped building with the black tape on the windows.

"Why did he want to see your hands?" Heather asked, leaning over to kiss me, putting her hand on my crotch.

"I told him I was Jesus, and he wanted to see the scars," I told her.

She laughed.

"You are terrible," she said.

"That's not what you said before," I told her.

She pinched my cheek like I was her fair haired boy and opened the door on her side.

"Let's start pouring some fucking Jack" she said.

Once we were inside the old dance hall room which fed off into some small bedrooms, we sat up the coolers with ice and beer and Coke. Then we set up the bottles. Everyone wrote his name on his bottle so nobody would be siphoning off booze when his bottle got low. It was standard practice Stan assured me early in the year. Then someone hooked up an old record player, and we listened to the Beatles while the various couples danced a little or sprawled out on the five couches that were scattered there. I got a lot of ribbing about the motel guy and my hands. I told the story about my Jesus hands and they all laughed except for Stan's date, Barbie Cooper, who had taken too many pain killers before her first drink. She was a little bleary eyed and lay there like an extra throw pillow, her mini skirt hiked up until you could see her pink panties.

Someone lit a bong, and we had our second and third drink. Heather was rubbing herself against me, and someone turned off most of the lights. Bobby's date Rita started moaning really loud. I guess she wanted some attention.

"You sound like you are passing a kidney stone," somebody said.

I think it was Jere, the youngest of the Brooklyn Jews.

"Shut up, Fuck Face," Rita told him and then kept moaning but not as loud.

First, I could tell that Heather really wanted to do it, and then she changed her mind and started pushing me away. I was pretty drunk and also stoned, and the wrestling in slow motion turned into lying in each other's arms and going to sleep. The others were pretty quiet. Stan and Epstein took their dates off into separate bedrooms and shut the doors.

I woke up after midnight. My head hurt, and I had a pain in my shoulder from sleeping awkwardly. I made my way into the small kitchen and turned on a light, glad someone had the foresight to bring instant coffee. I lit a Winston and waited for the water to heat up in a saucepan. Out the window, I could see the wind moving the leaves. I heard something spooky, probably a coyote.

When the explosion of noise and screaming erupted, it sounded like two people falling out of bed. I thought one of the old iron bed steads had collapsed under the athletic activity on the mattress.

"You mother fucker! You damned worthless fuck!"

It was Barbie Cooper. Then Stan's voice.

"Shit. . . shut up! You bitch! It's okay!"

Sort of contradictory threads of words. I turned off the fire and walked into the main room and hit the light switch. Everyone was blinking their eyes and pawing the air like they had come out of some hypnotic trance. They were all still drunk and stoned. Most were looking at the door where Stan and Barbie were, like they were wondering what came next.

I ran over and pounded on the door with my fists.

"You guys okay?"

There was a pause. Then Stan.

"It's okay, Bobo. Butt out!"

It was a little conciliatory but mostly really pissed off. Then, just as I was backing away from the door, Barbie Cooper slammed out the door, her clothes in her hand. She was naked except for some panties, and there was blood down the back of her leg. I wanted to cover her up, but then Heather appeared beside me with an old green blanket and put it around her. Barbie hugged Heather and started moaning and wailing.

Stan stalked out, threw a glance at everyone and picked up a whiskey bottle he brought. He took off the top and put it to his lips and drank down three or four swallows, his gullet moving rhythmically, now half the bottle nearly gone.

"Goddam bitches anyway!" he growled and walked out

the back door.

Before we could figure out what came next, two of the girls had their coats on and they moved like troops on a mission, out the door, following Barbie and Heather. Touching Barbie in what must have been sisterly concern. Then We heard the old Volkswagen bus which Stan drove start up. By the time we got to the door, they were pulling out onto 641 on their way back to the college.

Coop and his girlfriend had just emerged from their room.

"What a party," Epstein said. "Fuckin' Stan really knows how to top off the night."

There was a silence then, like everyone had finally come into real time, and we were trying to make sense of it all.

"I am making me some coffee," I declared.

"Me, too, Bobo," two or three of them said.

After fifteen minutes, we all sat around that scarred green table, like a bunch of little kids, not knowing exactly what to make of it all. Several times, someone said something, like just a couple of words, and it was like a bunch of schizos talking and all of the words were not connected.

"You think we all are a part of this thing?" Jere asked, because he was the one who always worried the most, raised by his mom and his aunt and spoiled like he was a prince.

"Don't sweat it, Jere. It is just female shit. They will all go into the clinic with Barbie Cooper and we will have to talk to the Dears and lie our asses off."

"We won't get thrown out of school, will we?" Jere asked. "I don't want to die in Vietnam."

It was something which was there on the back burner for me, too.

"You got nothin' to worry about, Jere," Espstein told him. "You got flat feet."

Just then the door opens and the motel guy with the dingy undershirt comes in.

"Somebody fuckin' die?" he asked us.

"Nobody dead," I told him.

I had credibility because I was the callous guy.

He nodded.

"Good," he said. "I don't need a shit load of trouble."

"No trouble," Coop told him. "We are in the groove."

A couple of people gave nervous chuckles.

"That sounds like fuckin' hippy talk," the undershirt guy said.

Then everybody quit talking and sipped their coffee. The undershirt guy was almost to the bottom of his whiskey bottle and he took a sip.

"You damn kids are young," he told us. "You can do anything you want to."

He said in a kind of sad way like he was saying that we still had the chances he had missed.

"Me, I ain't got any options left," he said, and then he walked out the door.

"Should we got look for Stan?" I asked.

"No, he'll come back soon," Epstein said. "Fuckin' Stan ain't goin' nowhere."

I got another cup of coffee, and I could see just the hint of gray at the edge of the dawn.

Suddenly, I leaned back on one of the old couches, and I felt the night's fatigue well up in me. When I awakened a few hours later, I heard shouting outside. I got to the door and opened it. There was a state trooper car there, and a couple of beefy guys in trooper hats were talking to the motel guy.

The first thing I thought of was the booze which was illegal since we were nineteen, and then I thought of the weed. But the undershirt guy's hands were flying around like he was in a play, giving that final speech which summed everything up.

Then the three of them walked off down a path toward the river, and that was when I thought of Stan.

"Oh, shit!" I said out loud.

Epstein and Jere walked out the door a little groggily.

"Fuckin' Stan show up?" Epstein asked, yawning as he lit up a Marlboro.

We all walked back into the big room and checked all the little rooms and cubby holes. I hoped he would be there wrapped in a blanket, snoring like he sometimes did.

"No fuckin' Stan," Jere announced as we all came together.

We went outside and watched down the long path where the three men stood huddled together on the shore, looking down at something we could not see. We started down the path, barefoot on rocks and sand.

"Shit! Shit! Shit!" said Epstein.

One of the troopers, a crew cut with a big gut, met us fifty feet from the edge of the river.

"You know anything about this?" he asked, like he was mad, like he hated drunk college kids and all the stupid shit they did.

The way we all looked around at each other, if I were him, I would have guessed that the bunch of us killed Stan and threw him in the river.

"Is he dead?" Jere asked in that kind of fearful voice he sometimes got, three octaves higher than usual.

"He is pretty fuckin' dead, kid," the trooper said.

Then.

"You want to tell me what happened?"

Epstein stepped forward. He was the least drunk of us all, and he had a loud Brooklyn voice that had some swagger in it, like he was telling you the truth.

He told it all. The motel money. The booze. The party. The girls. Barbie Cooper. Stan going off mad and drunk.

"You think he drowned himself on purpose?" the trooper asked, his voice weary as though he had done this too often, all the mess, all the tragedy, all the stupidity, over and over

"That doesn't sound like Stan," I said. "He was . . . kind of . . . full of himself."

The trooper looked around and the others nodded. Then the sheriff came up and the two of them huddled away from us. I sat down on a rock. It was coming to me now, how big this was, how I had not ever been a part of anything like this.

Then the trooper got on his car mike and called in.

"It's a drunk college kid who drowned," he said. "No, we don't know if he meant to do it. Maybe got drunk and got mad at his girlfriend and went for a swim. That's going to be my call. Save his parents a little grief."

Then he turned his back to us and talked some more. I was guessing it was about Barbie Cooper and what happened between them.

Then the motel guy came out and started this long ramble about how he rented it to us for a quiet party, that he didn't know anything about the booze and underage drinking. It sounded like bull shit to me, but if I was the undershirt guy, I guess I would have said the same thing. He was swearing and stamping his foot.

Then the sheriff put an arm around his shoulder.

"The kid is dead, Willie. You don't need to yell. The kid was from New York. We know college kids lie. Just go inside and calm down. Get Ethel to fry you up some eggs and bacon."

So, Willie, the owner goes back inside, mumbling to himself.

"You kids sober enough to drive," the sheriff said to us

He could tell a few of us were still pretty drunk, but we told him we could drive. I knew he just wanted to get us out of the way. He had our campus dorm addresses and phone numbers.

"Leave the booze," he said, his eyes roaming from one to the next.

We drove back, following each other, just like a funeral procession, I thought to myself.

Back at my dorm room, I tried to sleep but my nerves were all jangled, and I kept seeing Stan lying there under that tarp. After a while, I dropped off and I dreamed of Stan.

He stood in the doorway of our shared bathroom. He was standing in his underwear with his fat gut hanging over the waist band.

"It don't mean shit, Bobo," he told me with that funny smile he had.

When I woke up, I could see it was nearly nighttime. I pulled on a Stones' shirt and some cutoff jeans. I walked over to the cafeteria and got last in line. I took some meatloaf and green beans and some iced tea. I sat by myself and tried not to look anybody in the eye.

A guy named Wesley came over who knew Jere and Stan and Epstein.

"Fuckin' Stan is dead, man," he said. "That ain't right."

I nodded to him.

"Yeah, it ain't right," I told him and he walked off back to his table.

I ate a little put it on the cleaning tray. The janitor was putting chairs on the table so he could mop.

I drove off onto a bunch of country roads and found a little picnic table by a creek. The air smelled like wood smoke, and it reminded me of the times my father and I burned plant beds in March.

Big walls of fire and smoke with popping sounds as the fire reached wet knots of wood.

I thought how Stan was just mostly all bluff and loud

words, and I tried to think of him standing there at the edge of the river and then jumping in to solve something he could not make sense of.

A farm truck came by with rattling quarter panels.

"You okay, son," a voice came to me, an older farmer smoking his pipe.

"Yes, sir. I had a death in the family," I lied because it was something he would understand.

"Well, I am sorry for that. It happens all the time, but it ain't easy, is it?"

Then he patted my shoulder and got in his truck and drove off.

That was when I started to cry. I sat there crying, and it started raining a little. I thought of Stan that first day when we introduced ourselves, and he smiled big with that cleft chin and said, "Let me tell you something, mother fuckers. I am the cock of the walk."

Then he laughed big, and we all did. We ate our meals together in the cafeteria, and we played Spades at night. I went to the library more than the rest of them. I would leave at six and they were playing Spades. I would come back at 10:00 when the library closed, and they were playing spades, three or four of them smoking cigarettes. Stan was nearly always in an undershirt and some pajama bottoms.

"Look, it is Bobo, the scholar, come down to talk to the piss ants," he said, smiling at me.

"Say something, Bobo."

Everyone looked up.

"Hello, piss ants," I said, and Stan led the chorus of laughter.

Since Stan was twenty-four, he bought everyone beer and liquor. Some of the older guys always charged three or four dollars extra for their trouble, but Stan would have none of that.

"I got to have fuckers to get drunk with," he said. "Getting drunk ought to be cheap."

The rain got heavier and I got into my car and drove past a little Tennessee bar where an old bored guy sold me a six pack of Falstaff. I drank it as I drove back to the college, throwing the empty bottles in the ditches. When I walked into the dorm room, there it looked like a convention. All my roommates, the college cops, the sheriff and two of three official looking people which I took to be the dean or his subordinates.

When I walked in, everyone stopped and looked up. I stood watching them, wondering if I should turn around and get in my car and drive home to my parents' house. I was pretty sure I was no longer a college student.

But one of the college cops said, "Come on in, son. We

just have some questions to ask you."

I was sure the others had already answered the same questions. I told why we went to the Delux Accom. I lied a few times, but mostly it was the truth. All of my friends were watching me closely, and I wondered how many versions the cops had heard that night.

When the door opened, we all turned. There was this man with a mustache and an expensive suit, and there was a woman with a mink coat on and lots of rings and necklaces.

"Who knows why my son is dead?" she asked.

Her voice was cold and angry. Then she started to cry which turned into a kind of banshee howl and got louder and louder. Stan's old lady was going off the deep end. I edged toward the door.

The state trooper and the dean started to tell her the story, and they got a little mixed up when they got to Barbie Cooper and what might have happened there.

"Tell me where that bitch is," Stan's mom said loudly "I want to see the girl who killed my son."

Then three or four people were talking at once. I opened the door and slipped away.

Outside the dorm, walking toward my car, I could hear her voice getting louder and louder. It got quiet for a moment and she made that long, low sound like a wounded creature who thinks the world has turned cold and bad and it would not ever get any better, ever, ever.

When I backed out, I could still hear Stan's mom screaming and making that awful noise, a noise like you would make after words were no good, a noise like dying would be the next thing and it would be better than trying to go on when the heart was maimed and the soul was slain and nothing would fix it.

Jim Gish

Jim Gish was born and raised in Western Kentucky in the relentless forge of the Southern Baptist Church. Gish graduated from Murray State University, attended Law School at the University of Dayton and then received a Master's Degree in Counseling. He has taught high school and college for forty-nine years. He is a writer, a college instructor in psychology and a counselor. His oldest daughter Elizabeth received her Ph D from Harvard University and his youngest daughter Kathleen received her Ph D from The University of Cincinnati.

Gish lives in a hundred-year-old farmhouse in Arcanum, Ohio, with his fiancé Teri and their two cats, Buttons and Annabelle.

A Day with 3D
By Anne Hill

"You'll like New Zealand," said my mother's well-travelled friend, as I tucked in a last few items before leaving for Orlando Airport. "I found the New Zealanders so friendly and old-fashioned," she continued, "a bit like we Americans were in the 1930's."

A day later, weary and clinging to that comforting thought, I finally exited an Air New Zealand jet in the land I'd dreamed for years of visiting, having traveled thousands of miles from my native Florida.

I arrived with a mission. In January 1970, New Zealand needed me.

The previous year, I had learned of the country's desperate shortage of educators, which meant that schools often hired staff who were not fully qualified. The problem was particularly acute in Southland Province where there were at least sixty-three openings. This was my chance. Recently graduated with an MFA in Theatre, plus a degree in English and a year's successful experience teaching; I applied to The New Zealand Ministry of Education, sending in my resume and transcripts.

Almost immediately, I received an offer from Southland College in Invercargill, a city at the very tip of the South Island. My contract would classify me as a "Relieving Teacher," instructing classes in English and Dramatics beginning in February of 1970.

Pictured on the prospectus was a photograph of the college, actually a secondary school. Immense, gray, and three stories high, the school had opened in 1912 and looked anything but welcoming. Undeterred, I accepted at once, obtained a long-term visa, and made plans to leave the following January, a week before the opening of classes.

I was excited by the chance to see this young country. I also wanted to make a real contribution while I was there. Perhaps it might even be possible to start an after-school theatre group for young people.

However, after landing and meeting the headmaster, Ron Corker, it became immediately clear that it would take all my energy simply to get through each day. I was assigned seven different classes, with only four planning periods during the week.

Those four periods were conditional. I might have to use all of them to fill in for another teacher if that teacher had an emergency or was ill. Schools in Southland did not have the luxury of being able to call on substitute teachers. No days had been allotted for teacher planning before the students arrived. I would have to start cold on opening day in a system completely unfamiliar to me. That day arrived on February 3, 1970. Apprehensive but determined not to show it, I walked from my nearby flat to Southland College to join new colleagues. Together, we would greet nearly a thousand children.

Bright sunlight poured through tall windows on the second-floor teachers' lounge where we gathered. I sat very still, dressed to impress. Poised for the formal opening of school, I kept reminding myself to show confidence. The right clothes seemed to help. I wore my best suit and smiled. Inside, I felt more like a raw recruit awaiting transport to a boot camp renowned for excessive brutality.

With the rest of the faculty, including two fellow Americans, I listened for the tread of the headmaster and rose when he charged in, a general primed for battle. Arrayed for maximum intimidation, Ron Corker wore a black robe, and carried a Bible. The unspoken message was clear. Feckless youth must be disciplined and educated. Today the struggle would begin anew, as evidenced by students waiting noisily below, energy barely contained by a few staff.

"C'mon, follow me...they're all down there waiting," he ordered, his face as stern as an Old Testament prophet on the Vatican ceiling. Descending steps to a cavernous assembly room on the ground floor, trailing the black robe that billowed behind him like smoke from a diesel engine, I and the other teachers followed.

I struggled to catch up. Somehow, breathless from nerves, I found my way onstage to one of the chairs placed for teachers. Meanwhile, Corker, still on a march, reached a lectern placed downstage. Silence fell like a massive weight.

"Good Morning, Pupils," spoke Corker, in a tone of command.

"Good Morning, Mister Corker," chorused the students.

"A reading from the Bible," intoned Corker, opening the Bible with great solemnity. "Psalm 12," he read. "Help, Lord; for the godly man ceaseth."

As he continued, my own thoughts also turned heavenward, in hopes of divine intervention. Today I would meet hundreds of students, and I had never felt so unprepared. I had no class schedule. I had not met the Head of the English Department, reportedly unwell. I had no syllabus. I had even been prevented from reviewing the textbooks my students might be using. They remained locked in cabinets until I could distribute them.

Immediately before me stood a sea of twelve and thirteen-year-old girls in blue cotton dresses with Peter Pan collars and short sleeves. A snatch of song from "The Sound of Music" about girls' dresses briefly crossed my mind, but I knew instantly that these clothes would never be anyone's favorite things. The style seemed suited to young children rather than to youthful, developing bodies.

Behind the youngest girls, third form boys stood glumly, their expressions mirroring the monotony of their uniforms: shirts, sweaters, and short shorts with knee socks, all in gray. Alongside the walls stood rows of older students, mostly serious girls in white shirts and dark jumpers. Were these prefects? What exactly was a prefect?

"Open your hymn books," intoned Corker, nodding to the music teacher, Miss Christie. "We shall now sing "Guide Me On, Thy Great Redeemer."

With the rest of the faculty I stood and tried hard to mouth the words of the unfamiliar song, feeling for the first time The Church of England's grip on the country's culture. Ready to sit back down, I was quickly reminded of a second omnipresent institution, British royalty.

"Staff remain standing," ordered Corker, "Miss Anne Phillips, one of our new American teachers, will lead us in singing the national anthem."

Oh, God, what was it? Mercifully, Miss Christie, possibly mistaking the request, rescued me by playing an intro to "My Country 'Tis of Thee," the same melody as "God Save the Queen."

Britain's national anthem I could deal with. I sang out

and faked the words I didn't know.

Whew.

My relief was short lived. Girls' Headmistress Cecily Pierce came to the lectern. "Stay in your groups," she commanded. "Line up behind your teacher and go to your first period class."

With the other teachers, I left the stage in preparation to lead students to a classroom. Where was mine? I heard my name called but knew that my map couldn't help me. All the old room numbers had been painted over and changed. I was going to have to leave my group and ask Mrs. Pierce.

"We don't have a room yet for you, Miss Phillips. Mr. Neville is on leave, and you can use his in the meantime," she barked, before turning away without indicating either the room number or the direction.

Beside me, a tall man with a Scottish accent said, "I'll help you Miss Phillips. I teach English, too. M' name's McCrosstie."

And with that, he left his own group to guide me, along with thirty-eight giggly third formers, to a wooden portable. I had my first class, 3D Girls. I also had chaos.

"Please take your seats," I called helplessly, as nearly forty shrill voices joined in clamorous cacophony while continuously jumping around the room and changing desks. I had lost them already. I was on their turf. They knew it was unfamiliar to me and that I was new. I would have to fight hard for control. Where was some chalk? I found a small nub and wrote my name on the board, deciding to try an appeal.

"Hey, can you help me out? I'm new, and you're the only ones who can right now. We really need to get to know each other."

I began to get the attention of a few, although most continued to ignore me and stayed on their feet, jostling one another and loudly sharing a common crush on Jim Connelly, the new American science teacher.

"Oh, Gawd ain't 'e gorgeous?'

"Can't wait till I get 'im for science."

"But we might get the wife instead…she's supposed to teach, too." (Chorus of disappointed words, i.e."Aw, hell.")

"I'll put in for a transfer." (Hoots of laughter)

"Fat lot that'll get you with Pierce…and don't let 'er catch you with ya skirt tucked up that way."

"She's just outside! I see 'er commin," yelled a large blonde girl by the door.

And in a twinkling, I stood before a demure group of rapidly seated young ladies, who looked at me expectantly.

Cecily Pierce peeked in, nodded and went on, amid suppressed giggles from the class. I allowed myself to smile and silently blessed her.

No one had given me a list of enrollments. After a brief introduction, I invited the girls to begin introducing themselves, one at a time. At first, no one stirred. Amid whispers and giggles, a tall girl on the front row slowly stood, dark, tangled hair hiding most of her face. Her head hung down and I glimpsed a nervous smile as she began, haltingly, to speak.

"M'name's Raewyn McPeek, n' I live in Bluff, an' me uncle calls me a mongrel 'cause me mum's from Samoa an' m'dad's from Aussie."

From the back of the room came, "Hey, Rae, you got a lotta uncles I hear come t' y' house when ya dad's away."

Ear-splitting laughter followed as Raewyn stood defiantly, looking back at the apparent speaker, fists clenched.

"Thank you, Raewyn, for starting us off. You get to pick who goes next."

Transformed by new and unaccustomed power, Raewyn lifted her head, straightened her shoulders, and pointed to the student who'd made the jibe.

"Her!" she said triumphantly, continuing to stand while a short, round-faced brunette mumbled a name I could not understand.

"Thanks, Raewyn. You may sit down now."

"Betcha she doesn't want to say 'er name," muttered

Raewyn, sinking into her seat.

"Excuse me," I said to the brunette, "but I didn't understand your name. Could you repeat it, please?"

"Christine."

"I need you to give me your last name, please."

"It's Smellie," she said, almost spitting out the two words as if daring others to laugh. Ignoring a growing chorus of snickers, she continued with increasing volume," It's S-M-E-L-L-I-E!"

"Good for you, girl," I thought silently, before saying, "Thank you, Christine. That was helpful. Please choose the next person, and we will continue."

And so we did, managing to get through over half of the class before a loud bell sounded.

"Interval," shouted a girl who'd just introduced herself as "Maree." As she moved towards the door, the rest followed noisily en masse, leaving me feeling as empty as the old classroom.

The girls seemed to know exactly where to go, which was more than I did until "McCrosstie" poked his head inside my open classroom door.

"C'mon upstairs to morning tea, lass," he said.

In the middle of the teachers' lounge, a large trolley groaned under the weight of scones, cream cakes, savories, and finger sandwiches. At the back of the room, a line formed for cups of hot tea from a large dispenser. Choosing sandwiches, I looked for Jim and Judy Connolly in the large room where faculty, mostly middle aged, had draped themselves over chairs with the weary familiarity of soldiers long sharing the same trench. By one of the windows, I spotted Jim and Judy, and perched beside them on the worn arm of a chair. In the rueful smiles we exchanged was an understanding which needed no words: Southland College was one rough school.

Between bites of my sandwich, I heard Mrs. Pierce raise her voice over the chit-chat and ask for attention. "Faculty, please make sure enrollment forms are returned to the office by the beginning of lunch."

Again, I found myself an exception. "Mrs. Pierce, I never received an enrollment form for 3D Girls."

"Forms were sent around to every teacher's room."

"I don't have a room assigned to me yet."

"That was an omission. I'll see that your enrollment form is in your box for tomorrow. In the meantime, hand in a list of all the names in your class."

Anticipating a rowdy return from interval, I went back to my classroom early, surprised to find the room no longer empty. In one corner sat a small, slight Asian girl, head bowed.

"Hello, is anything wrong?"

Without looking up, she silently shook her head.

"Can you tell me your name?"

I saw her nod and heard a faint "Anna," just as the bell signaled a noisy reentry of her classmates.

All over again, I had to fight for their attention and continue to gather names. But at last, just as the bell rang, I was able to add the final student's name to class enrollment before heading upstairs for lunch. There, one more assignment waited.

"Faculty, I need your attention!" demanded Pierce. "For the rest of the afternoon, students will be outdoors playing sport. You will supervise and referee the activity to which you are assigned. Miss Phillips, you will referee girls' cricket."

"Mrs. Pierce, I know nothing about cricket."

"The girls will teach you."

"Then shouldn't one of them referee?"

"I'll assign someone else to referee cricket. You can coach shot put and discus."

"Excuse me, Mrs. Pierce," said Mr. McCrosstie. "I can use Miss Phillips' help in organizing the boys' and girls' races."

"Very well, Mr. McCrosstie."

Again, I had reason to be grateful for his kindness. As we sat side by side, cheering young runners, I ventured a question.

"Mr. McCrosstie, what does the letter after a class mean? Two of my classes are marked "D.""

"It means the students are at the bottom of their class in ability and achievement. They know they're not likely to go higher or to pass School Certificate."

Inside, I had already known the answer, but hoped I was wrong. Was the sense of failure really locked in so early? I resolved to search continually for fresh ways to inspire each student. In the meantime, I could start by helping pupils like Anna, one at a time. She seemed so alone. I knew how that felt.

With plans to discover Anna's background, I headed back to the teachers' lounge as school ended, intending to start inquiries the next day. Surprisingly, I did not have to wait that long. Cecily Pierce had reminded me at morning tea that I had a box. I checked and found my enrollment form there as promised. Beneath lay something else, a small folded paper that I nearly discarded before seeing "Miss Phillips" written carefully in pencil on the outside fold. Opening the sheet, I read,

"Dear Miss Phillips,

I am Anna Dockery's mother. Me and my husband adopted Anna from an orphanage in China six years ago. We do not know exactly how old she is. She is shy and can't read

good. If you could help her improve, it would be appreciated.

Yours faithfully,

Thelma Dockery"

In asking for my assistance, Mrs. Dockery could not have known what a lift she gave me. I welcomed a chance to work with this gentle girl. We both just survived our first day at a tough school, and though Anna did not know it yet, she would no longer struggle alone.

Anna came to my classroom the next day to work on her reading, an after-school pattern that continued regularly throughout the first school term. By the time the term ended in May, both her reading ability and her confidence had dramatically improved. She now smiled often. And so did I. Gradually, the quality of Anna's work became level with her classmates, often surpassing them. Within the same time period, my own struggles lessened, and I gained a sense of control over my workload.

I remained in New Zealand not for one year, but for seventeen, long enough to see needed reforms come to New Zealand schools after I married a New Zealander, reforms that were to benefit my two New Zealand-born children, now American citizens.

Though my family now lives happily in the United States, the lovely land nicknamed by native Kiwis, "Land of the Long White Cloud," still calls us now and then to visit and see again the wonders of snowy alps, the beauty of jewel-like lakes, the majesty of fjords rising from the sea and, yes, a once dilapidated old school, now over a hundred years old.

Southland College, now Southland Technical College, endures, greatly and wonderfully expanded and modernized, the pride of Southland Province. Most urgently of all, New Zealand calls us back to renew contact with beloved friends and relatives, many found during that first difficult year in Invercargill.

My mother's friend was right. She said I would like New Zealand. And I did.

Anne Hill

Anne Hill lives in the vibrant college town of Gainesville, Florida, with her beloved rescue dog, Daphne. She is the proud mother of a daughter who works for the University of Florida and a son who is an army colonel and physician.

During her years in New Zealand, she taught theatre and speech in her home, directed children's plays, and helped run a theatre program at Waikato University on New Zealand's North Island.

Returning to the United States, she taught speech in a community college while embracing the drama of life as a hospital social worker.

Currently, while working on a memoir, she enjoys being part of a community health initiative, an active writer's alliance in Gainesville, and a joyfully challenging dance class.

Welcome to Vietnam
By Chuck Jackson

Have you ever looked at a blank piece of paper or computer screen and imagined, if written, what the words would say? What if they were words about yourself, and people from your life? What if it was something you concealed because it was horrible or too revealing to discuss, let alone write about? How would you begin, and what would you say?

For anyone who reads this, I will fill the blank pages with a period of my life I wanted to forget. It was a time that took me from immaturity, immersed me into the reality of adulthood, and forced me to make decisions I was ill equipped to make. It was a time when my perception of humanity was shattered while I chased an ambition solely to overcome my low self-esteem.

I fill these pages with experiences, emotions, and the individuals who changed me. They contain details of horrors of an indefensible war, where the commanders put their men into reckless jeopardy. This was a war where the heroes returned home in dishonor and shame. A war where many paid the ultimate sacrifice because of the careless disregard for human life.

When I returned from Vietnam, I felt the honor that I'd served. But, like so many of my Vietnam Veterans, I kept my honor suppressed. I kept those memories repressed until I shared this and other stories. My reason for writing my story now is to bring purpose, validity, and honor to those individuals I served with and who are portrayed in my writings.

HH-43B (Pedro) in the foreground with a Douglas A-1 (Sandy) in the background

* * *

In December 1968, after completing 14 months of Special Forces training to be a member of the Air Force Pararescue team (PJ), I left my wife in tears and joined a hundred plus men from all branches of the military for the dreaded flight to Vietnam. Dressed in our fatigues, we boarded the aircraft at Travis AFB with stops in Alaska, Japan and then on to Vietnam. The closer we got to Da Nang, the more nervous we became.

Upon our arrival, the weather was cold and rainy; the scene was bedlam, with aircrafts of all sorts and sizes parked haphazardly. Military vehicles of various types were running back and forth-carrying men, fuel and cargo. Over to the side, I spotted a haunting site I would never forget. Lined up were many baggage carts, and on them were black bags containing the bodies of men who had given their lives. I saw no honor guard, nor flag covered caskets; only those body bags lying in the freezing rain.

* * *

When I checked into the 38th ARRS (Aerospace Rescue and Recovery Service) Detachment 7 in Da Nang, they assigned me to an Air Force Kaman HH-43B team. The HH-43B "Huskie" or as PJs named it "Pedro" they never designed it for combat because of its slow speed, short range, and it was not armored.

My team included Air Force Major William (Billy) Atkins, First Lieutenant Lawrence (Larry) Riley, Airman Samuel (Sammy) Burkowitz, and me. Our call name was Pedro 7-5. The other three had been together for several months and I was replacing a PJ that had rotated back stateside.

The first week we did nothing but Medevac to get me broken in. Although I was told this was temporary, my ignorance of actual rescue missions left me bored and wanting more. I did not understand what my future held; however, it wasn't long before they immersed me into the reality of being a PJ.

I was hanging out in Detachment 7's ready room with Sammy when the alarm sounded. By the time we arrived at our bird, Billy had the engines running and Larry was standing out front watching for us. As soon as I got out of the vehicle, Larry yelled, "Come on Doc. Get your gear on; we need to be in the air." Sammy and I didn't have enough time to get anymore than our helmets on and plugged into the communication systems when Billy was lifting off.

I asked, "What's the scoop?"

Larry said, "We got two Huey medivac birds down. Sandy 2-7 says he is not sure there were survivors. There are hostiles crawling all over the area and command has scrambled a support jet and a second Sandy from Dak To."

"Are we the only rescue crew?"

Billy said, "No, Pedro 4-4 out of Pleiku will be in support, but we are the primary." Billy snickered, "Hey Doc, I hope you put on clean skivvies this morning. You wanted a mission, you got one now."

Within 20 minutes, we were in communication with

Sandy 2-7. He all but escorted us over to the crash site. We were circling at 1,000 ft. and it did not look good. Wreckage was spread over a quarter mile, although one cabin seemed to be intact. It took another half-hour of circling in the distance, with the two Sandy's and an F-100 Super Sabre clearing the area. Pedro 4-4 was in formation with us.

Finally, we got the call, "Pedro 7-5, Sandy 2-7; Copy? ."

Larry answered, "This is Pedro 7-5; Go ahead."

They gave us the green light and Billy made the turn. We heard the Sandy, tell Pedro 4-4 to maintain his pattern. Billy made a wide sweep and then as he lowered to less than 200 ft. Sammy yelled, "We got some hostiles at 7 o'clock." Billy instantly kicked our bird in the butt and ascended back to 1,000 ft.

"Pedro 7-5, this is Rooster nine-err, two—two. Maintain your altitude."

Billy replied, "10-4, Rooster 9-2-2; Roger that."

Out of nowhere, a F-100 swooped in below us and hit the area with an onboard rocket followed by his guns. The target lit up with flames and smoke.

Sandy 2-7 cleared us again for an approach. This time we saw nothing, and Billy brought us in, hovered at six ft., and I jumped. Billy immediately rose and was making tight sweeps. I ran toward the cabin. When I got within 100 yards, I started seeing body parts. While still strapped I found the pilot in the cockpit, the other two were lying outside at various distances. The body parts seemed to come from one individual.

I radioed, "Pedro 7-5, PJ 7-5; Copy?"

Larry responded, PJ 7-5; Go ahead.

"No survivors here. Give me the direction to the other site."

"PJ 7-5, 3 o'clock and 200 meters."

"10-4"

I hightailed over toward the other site. I had to break through some thick brush. Once I did, I saw a burned cabin, or what was left of the cabin. I also saw severely burned bodies. I only found what I could identify as two crew members.

"Pedro 7-5, PJ 7-5; Copy?"

"PJ 7-5; Go ahead."

"No survivors here. Check on the number on board this Huey."

"PJ 7-5; Roger that."

While I waited, I searched the area. The stench from the burned bodies was nauseating. I checked in all directions, finding nothing.

"PJ 7-5, Sandy 2-7; Copy?"

"Sandy 2-7; Go ahead."

"Command says crew of three on each bird. Copy?"

"10-4, Sandy 2-7; thank you."

Billy instructed me to return to the first site. He said Pedro 4-4 would handle the burned site.

With both Sandy's, keeping watch over our backsides, Billy landed at the first site. He kept our bird's engines running. Sammy helped me get the pilot out and put him in a body bag. We gathered as many body parts as we could find and put them in a separate bag. We did not have another bag, so we used a tarp out of our emergency locker and wrapped the third crewmember. Then we loaded all three in our bird.

Pedro 4-4 landed at site two and it took its crew 30 minutes to find the third crewmember. We left before Pedro 4-4 and headed for our base. For the last week, I had hauled body bags when we did Medevac. However, this seemed more dismal. Perhaps it was because these were flight crews and not Army grunts. No one spoke on the return to base.

As I helped unload our formidable cargo, I must have had a melancholy appearance. Billy walked over, put his arm around me, and said, "I'm sorry to tell you Doc, it doesn't get any easier." Then, cynically, he added, "Oh yeah, Welcome to Vietnam."

Thoughts of a Pararescueman

I am that which others do not want to be. I chose to go where others fear and excel where they have failed.

I ask for nothing from those that will not give... and reluctantly accept the thought of eternal loneliness, ...should I fail.

I have seen the face of death, felt the stinging cold of fear; I have realized the harsh reality of just what this job is all about. I enjoyed the sweet taste of victory and love; but those were just fleeting moments.

I have cried, pained and hoped, most of all, I have lived times others would say are best forgotten...But,

At least I will be able to say that I was proud of who and what I am and that in my heart and soul I will always be a "PJ"   *<Unknown author>*

"These Things We Do, That Others May Live,"

Chuck Jackson

Chuck Jackson is a retired accountant living in Southeast Florida. He was an 'Air Force Brat' and followed his dad's 33-year military career by also serving four years in the Air Force.

He is an extensive reader and since retirement; he has spent much of his time studying and enhancing his love for writing. This story is taken in part from his published memoir. He is a two-time cancer survivor and draws his strength from his faith and church activity.

For years, he spoke little of his Vietnam experience, suffering similarly as many Vietnam Veterans anguished in silence. With this writing, he wants to help return the honor and dignity of those that served with him. He dedicates this story to those men that proudly served as PJs.

Thanks Mussolini
By Richard Key

It's 1996 and we're on a train in Italy headed to Bari, my wife's birth city. This is a once-in-a-lifetime voyage that I've been dreaming about and planning for the past six months. We depart out of Rome's Termini station into the bucolic countryside traveling diagonally from the west coast to the east coast, from the Lazio region to Apulia. Bari is situated on the Adriatic Sea where the spur would be attached if the boot of Italy had a spur. It's May and the verdant hills are in full bloom. The first-class train accommodations have compartments that fit our group of six perfectly. There are no open seats for strangers to fill. No need for fake politeness. Just us. And we can spread out and relax.

But, there's one problem. The air-conditioning is out in the car I reserved, so we open up the window which keeps enough air circulating for us to survive. Unfortunately for me, though, all the pollen from the Italian peninsula blows in and contains something that sets off a massive hay fever attack. I'd like to think the offending agent is the pollen of some delicate Tuscan olive or grape, but it's probably something like Sicilian snotweed. Trouble is, I hadn't thought to bring antihistamines on the trip. How could I be allergic to something in Europe?

When we arrive in Bari, all our Kleenex tissues are gone. My eyes are red, and I'm wiping my nose on anything that's not wet or moving. I've lost two pounds in mucus. We present ourselves to the Palace Hotel, where I'm sure I don't make a very good impression on the staff. And there's no record of our reservation. The desk clerks hold my papers up to the light and chat together in their melodic tongue. Business was slow, so they shrug their shoulders and decide they might be able to spare a room or two. We explain that my wife was born in their fair city, and this was the hotel that her parents stayed at when they first arrived back in the fifties. A native! The clerks brighten up and offer to accommodate us in upgraded rooms with a complimentary breakfast. For the record, this was also before the era of the Eurozone. Lira was the national currency, with an exchange rate of just under 1,600 lira per dollar. The hotel lets us have rooms for 240,000 lira that are normally 420,000. Lira made you feel rich. I miss lira.

My condition improves after going to a *farmacia* and somehow piercing the language barrier with the pharmacists to obtain my antihistamine Seldane. *Antistaminico? Seldane? Per allergie? Antistaminico?* Finally, a light goes on when I print the name on the back of our city map: *Ah si! Teldane! Si!* The medicine in Italy is spelled with a "t" and pronounced "tell Donnie."

To some people, 1996 may sound like the Stone Age, and in some ways it was a bit primitive. Traveling back then was certainly a far different experience than it is now. For one thing, it was possible to get lost, something that cell phones and GPS have largely done away with. The present-day traveler always knows where he or she is and how to get back. They may occasionally be off the grid, or their batteries may be running low, but they know that their modern gadgets will save them in the end. They depend on it. It's like having the answers to a quiz on the back page. You know you can cheat if it comes down to it. It wasn't always so.

This was the first time my wife, Laurie, and I had ever been out of the country. Our two children, six and eight, were coming along, and I invited my in-laws, whom we referred to as Grammie and Poppie, to accompany us. They lived in Bari for a couple of years in the late fifties where my father-in-law worked as a petroleum geologist for Cities Service. I say it was our first trip out of the country, but Laurie, of course, was born (poetically) in Bari, so this was a return trip for her to see her city of origin (she was one year old when they returned to the US) and also to let her parents relive some of their glory days.

One used to require a travel agent to book hotels

overseas, and it took a certain amount of faith. You seldom had photographs or customer ratings to guide you. Then you had to keep up with a stack of printouts as proof to hoteliers that you had a reservation or had prepaid some part of the cost. I used an agency called Fair Winds Travel close to where I worked. Faxes and phone calls were considered state of the art. Maps and guidebooks were essential.

At that time, the Internet was in its infancy and few businesses had websites. You had to purchase plane tickets over the telephone, after which they came in the mail and you guarded them with your life. You bought train tickets directly at the station, waiting at the window, hoping that the few words you could speak in another language would be sufficient.

After tooling about Bari for a couple of days, my in-laws want to revisit a picturesque village south of the city called Alberobello, which consists of unique rounded white limestone dwellings called *trulli* with uniformly conical gray stone roofs. The only way to get there is to rent a car and drive the thirty miles. We find the place, deciphering the road signs as best we can. The village is much as they remembered it except that now there's a web of telephone and electrical lines. Also, each dwelling has its own television antenna, which detracts from its otherworldly charm. Without modern fixtures Alberobello looks like something you might see on the planet Tatooine, but with the addition of metal and wires resembles a prehistoric trailer park.

I get the car back to Bari without incident, and our plan is to leave on the train the following day for Venice. The Palace Hotel is across town from the train station, so it makes sense to keep the car overnight and avoid hiring a taxi. My job is to drop everyone off at eight o'clock in the morning and return the rental to the Avis dealership three blocks away. I would then walk back to the train station and meet them. Which might have worked perfectly, except for the excruciatingly slow desk work at Avis by the single employee. I wait my turn patiently at first, and then become fidgety, as those in front of me languidly finish their business and the minutes click by.

With an eye on my watch, anxiety builds. The train is scheduled to leave at nine o'clock. They aren't dependable like Amtrak. You can't count on their being an hour or two late. As the legend goes, the one good thing Mussolini did was get the trains running on time. Finally, with only five or six minutes to spare, the paperwork is signed and I'm out the door, hightailing it to the train station. There, across six or seven rows of tracks, is my family, waving from the back of the train. Signs warn people not to cross the tracks. They are in Italian, but I understand what they mean, and I ignore them. I hop over all the intervening tracks and climb onto the train to Venice with seconds to spare.

But Laurie's dad is gone.

"Where's Poppie?"

"He just got off to look for you," Grammie said. "He didn't think you'd make it."

Poppie thought that if I got left behind, at least we could deal with it together. The trouble with that idea, though, was that I was the only one who knew the name of the hotel we were headed to and how to get there. Right on schedule, nine sharp, the train pulls out of the station. I find one of the train officials and, in a panic, blurt out something in half English and half French: *mon beau-père... not on train... left behind!* He gives me a bemused and perplexed look as he walks slowly away without comment. I have a small Italian phrasebook, but it's geared more toward ordering pizza and asking where the facilities are. It isn't much good for "my father-in-law never made it onto the train."

We find our compartment, another six-seater, and the five of us settle in. This was the era before cell phones, I should explain. Laurie's mom offers to get off at the next stop to try to call the Bari police on a pay phone and explain what happened. But we talk her out of it, thankfully, because that stop was all of five minutes, and she surely would have been stranded as well.

The rest of the journey is somber as we contemplate the options.

"Poor Poppie," our daughter laments. Her companion, a stuffed orange, cross-eyed Stegosaurus named Bumba agrees and sighs a loud and plaintive "Bummm," the only word in his vocabulary.

The first idea I have is for all of us to get off at the next stop and ride a bus or train back to Bari. We have Europasses that allow for six days of train travel in three countries during a two-month period. Any train travel in any direction on this day was already paid for. But there's no guarantee of a bus or train going where we need it to, and what if Poppie couldn't be found? Grammie is frustrated and begins to blot her eyes as she weeps silently. The kids and Bumba give her hugs and assure her that everything will be okay.

At some point between Bari and Bologna, we cross the Rubicon—the actual river. It's but a small stream now, and they say it's polluted. But, like Julius Caesar's army, we forge ahead. The die has been cast, and there is no turning back.

In Bologna, we change trains to head eastward. Our spirits are low and we are in no mood for squatters sitting in our reserved compartment. I show them our tickets and explain in the universal language of evictors that all six seats belong to us. Later, we find out that the workers whose job it was to post the names of the occupants on the window of each compartment were on strike, which is why passengers felt like they could sit anywhere they pleased. That also meant we had no proof that the sixth seat belonged to us. We want it to stay empty since we paid for it. And we don't need some interloper trying to make small talk. The squatters eventually get settled somewhere else but every so often one of them walks slowly by the window and peers in at us, the sourpuss *Americanos* guarding the seat of the unknown passenger. Eventually we let Bumba have Poppie's seat, which seems to appeal to his vanity, expressing a noble "Bum!" with his tapered nose tilting slightly higher in the air.

It's late afternoon when we arrive at San Lucia station in Venice, and it is a fantastic place to arrive by train as the setting sun illuminates the grand canal and the green-domed church, San Simeone Piccolo. It's a renaissance painting that invites you into its landscape. Plan A is to find the hotel and check in with all our stuff. I would then return to the train station, where I would inspect every incoming train for a tall, slender man with white hair and a bewildered look on his face. Hopefully, he would have gotten on a later train. All he knew was what city we were headed to. Most likely he had figured out that I had somehow gotten on the train. There is no plan B.

I camp out for hours, watching each train for the misplaced Poppie. Hundreds of passengers disembark and swarm past my observation point every thirty minutes or so. Finally, at ten o'clock, with only one or two trains remaining on the schedule, I see a familiar tall man in khakis and a short sleeve knit shirt step slowly out of the train.

"I've never been so happy to see anyone in my whole life!" he exclaims. How many men have heard *that* from their father-in-law? He had come to the same conclusion we had and purchased a second-class ticket. We make our way to the hotel, where he is greeted like the long-lost prodigal son.

The next train to Venice didn't leave until one o'clock, Poppie explains, and he decided to try and contact an old friend. When he and Laurie's mom lived in Bari, a sweet Italian couple, the Vallentes, had taken them under their wing and treated them like family. Vencenzo was the man's name, and after almost forty years of no communication, no letters or anything, Poppie tried to contact him with what little information he had. He thought he found the correct number to call, and Vencenzo's son answered. In a more perfect world, there would have been a happy reunion of old friends and a shared bottle of wine as they recalled their time together long ago. The gray cloud of our unfortunate separation would have had the silver lining of a recovered friendship.

But this is a less perfect world, alas, and Vencenzo's son was rude.

"Signor Vallente is ill and wishes to be left alone," he explained. "And don't call back." Poppie tried once more with as much explanation as he could muster and got the same result, only louder. It was a stark reminder that untended friendships may survive a lapse of ten or twenty years, but thirty-seven is pushing the limit.

Having our group reunited without the intervention of the police or the American consulate, we felt the empowerment and the gratitude that people without technology used to feel when things somehow worked out all right. Oh sure, things are easier now, and probably safer, and we wouldn't go back. But, you could make the argument that travel was more interesting back then.

"Bum!"

THE END

Richard Key

Richard was born in Jacksonville, Florida and grew up in Mississippi. He currently lives in Alabama with his wife, Laurie, a skilled potter. He attended medical school at the University of Mississippi, and his real job is surgical pathologist. He has been writing essays and short stories for about twelve years and several pieces have been published. One piece, The Last Hundred Days, about turning sixty, was nominated by Hawaii Pacific Review for a Pushcart Prize. His author website is: richardkeyauthor.com. Richard's other interests include playing the piano, traveling, reading, and biking, although his bicycle was recently stolen. He deserved it. He had a lock and didn't use it, choosing naively to trust his fellow humans to be decent. Last time for that.

Ahmed the Tailor
By Barbara Mujica

Ahmed hated Americans. He'd lost his young nephew
and two cousins during the early months of the invasion,
and he held the Americans responsible for the violence and
chaos that ravaged his country. He knew that Al-Qaeda
operatives, not Americans, had planted the bomb that had
blown up Yasin, a gangling sixteen-year-old with dreams of
becoming a politician. Zamir, on the other hand, had fallen
victim to an American sniper, and Hasan had died when a
car exploded at a checkpoint in Ramadi. None of this would
have happened if the Americans hadn't invaded Iraq,
thought Ahmed, and now, to make matters worse, some of
his Sunni brothers had switched sides. They had joined the
Sunni Awakening, supporting the Marines in their drive
against Al-Qaeda. According to these turncoats, Al-Qaeda
did even more harm than the Americans. It was Al-Qaeda
who terrorized the populace, they said, decapitating
children to intimidate their parents, blowing up schools
and marketplaces to keep people cowering in their homes.
Of course, they said, no one wanted foreigners overrunning
the land, but if you had to choose between the Americans

and Al-Qaeda, the Americans were the lesser of two evils.

Ahmed wasn't buying any of it. It was the Americans' fault, he kept saying. It was all the Americans' fault. No one was coming into his tailor's shop, and it was because in the middle of a war, the last thing people thought about was buying a new suit. And who had caused this stupid war, anyway? The Americans!

"Things will change," his wife, Kayoosh, told him. "Ramadi is more peaceful now. Soon people will buy." At least, that's what I imagine she said.

It was true that the streets were quieter. Now that the Awakening was taking hold and the U.S. government had sent more soldiers—the "surge," they called it—you could walk through the souk, or marketplace, without fear that a bomb might explode under your feet. Some of the neighbors even liked the Americans. The men in uniform handed out candy and soccer balls to the children, and a few of them had learned some Arabic.

"They're killers!" snarled Ahmed.

"In wartime, everybody's a killer," said Kayoosh calmly.

"Well, I hate them! Candy and soccer balls don't make up for the deaths of three blood relatives!"

"You may have to take up sewing *disdashas*."

"I'm not sewing *disdashas*," snapped Ahmed, referring to the long, kaftan-like garments worn by many Iraqi men and most women. "My father made top-quality, British-style suits, and his father before him. That's what I know how to do."

Ahmed sat in his shop and waited. He didn't go to the brotherhood meetings, where men talked about the Awakening and how best to keep Al-Qaeda away. He didn't associate with neighbors who informed Marines about who was harboring insurgents or stockpiling weapons. He just sat in his shop, surrounded by bolts of superb English wool, and waited.

No one came.

I didn't know Ahmed, of course. My son Ignacio told me about him on one of those rare occasions when he talked about his time in Iraq. He never told war stories—the kind they show on television, where Americans kick in doors and get the bad guys. I imagine Ignacio kicked in doors too, during his first deployment, but by his second tour, many Sunnis were cooperating with the Marines, and the Americans reciprocated by rebuilding the town. They constructed schools and souks, set up medical centers, repaved the streets, and painted the water tower. That gave Ignacio the chance to meet people and make friends—but not with Ahmed. Ahmed wouldn't talk to the Marines. He wouldn't allow his boys to play with the American soccer balls they handed out. When he saw the neighborhood children crowding around soldiers and trying out their English—"Hello, my name is Sham!" "Hello, I like candy!"—he walked by in a hurry. When he saw the Americans clowning around—plopping their helmets down on the heads of seven-year-olds, who squealed with glee—he looked away.

Ignacio had heard about Ahmed. He met periodically with the sheiks to discuss security concerns and building projects, and occasionally Ahmed's name came up. Ahmed the tailor, who hated Americans. Ahmed, who probably didn't have any information about Al Qaeda, but you could never tell. You had to be careful. People who held grudged could be dangerous.

Ignacio knew where Ahmed's shop was. It was in the souk, attached to his house, between the rug seller and the stall that sold cheap T-shirts.

"I think I'll pay him a visit," said Ignacio.

"Don't bother," said one of the elders. "He won't talk to you. He won't even let you in."

In my mind, I conjure up an image of Ahmed. I see a man of about forty, aged by war and worry. His face, an elongated oval. His skin, rutted copper. Short black hair, heavy eyebrows, moustache, cleft chin, lackluster forehead. Intelligent eyes that draw me in, the eyes of a seer lost in a revelation. A solid but disordered body, like that of a broken boxer.

I imagine Ignacio sauntering up to that unwelcoming house. He can see Ahmed, the gloomy tailor, through the shattered window. He can see the bolts of fabric, the outmoded sewing machine, the bobbins, the thimbles. He can see Ahmed's boys, aged eight and ten, playing with empty spools. Ignacio knocks.

Ahmed hesitates, then gets up to open the door. He might as well open it, he thinks, because Ignacio can kick it in if he wants to. Actually, Ignacio won't kick it in because that's all over now. The Awakening has mostly put an end to kicking in doors. Even so, in Ahmed's mind, you can never know about Americans, so he opens it.

"Good morning," says Ignacio in Arabic. "I'm Lieutenant Ignacio Montez."

Ahmed squints at him through twisted spectacles.

"I'd like to have a suit made."

"A suit?" I asked my son. "Did you need a suit? In Ramadi?"

"I needed him to let me in," said Ignacio. "I thought this was the most effective way."

Ahmed stares at Ignacio a long time. Ignacio assumes he is sizing up the situation, deciding whether to trust him. But no, Ahmed is taking mental measurements, calculating yardage. He is clearly seething, but a job is a job. He hasn t had a commission in months.

"Stand over here," he barks, pointing to a small platform in front of a filmy full-length mirror.

"It needs to be resilvered," says Ignacio in English, but Ahmed doesn't understand, and Ignacio doesn't know how to say it in Arabic.

Ignacio is wearing no weapons except a sidearm, but two Marines are standing guard outside the store in case of trouble. Once Ahmed begins maneuvering the measuring tape across his back, down his arm, down his leg, Ignacio is sure that there will be no trouble. The man is clearly a master, a perfectionist—slow, methodical, precise. He assesses Ignacio's shape and stance. He measures each leg separately.

"Sit down," says Ahmed. "You will choose fabric."

In addition to the bolts of fine English wool, there are books with sample swatches. Ahmed wants to know where the suit will be worn, whether it must be suitable for a temperate climate or snow or the desert, whether it will be for summer or winter. Does Ignacio want pure wool? Gabardine or merino? Herringbone or sharkskin? A silk blend? Lightweight wool is good for the warm weather, he explains. And what about the color? What about the price?

Ahmed wants the equivalent of three hundred dollars for the grey gabardine suit that Ignacio picks out. Ignacio knows that a made-to-order garment of fine wool could cost a thousand dollars back home, but he also knows that he has to bargain. Ahmed expects it. He won't respect the American if he doesn't put up a fight. A dollar is worth a little less than 2,000 dinars. Neither man wants to calculate the price in tens of thousands of dinars, so they agree to negotiate in U.S. currency.

"One hundred," offers Ignacio.

"That's ridiculous! I have a family to feed!" counters Ahmed.

"One hundred ten."

"You're insulting me! Two hundred ninety!"

The negotiations go on for over an hour, during which Ahmed orders his ten-year-old to bring tea. Finally, they agree on two hundred dollars.

"Come back in three days," says Ahmed.

"When I tried it on and looked in the mirror, I felt like some kind of a fashion model from the eighties," Ignacio told me. "The suit was gorgeous, exquisitely styled although a bit outmoded. After all, Ramadi isn't the style capital of the Middle East, and Ahmed didn't have access to the latest patterns. But crap, Mom, it fit perfectly!" He carried it back to base and hung it on a hanger on a hook on the wall.

Nothing changed. Ahmed continued to stay away from neighborhood meetings, and he continued to badmouth

Americans. When the neighborhood kids crowded around the Marines for candy and soccer balls, Ahmed's sons weren't among them.

A few weeks later, Ignacio trudged back down the road to the souk past rows of bullet-pocked houses. He noticed that some people had begun repairing walls and painting doors. There was no sense in making repairs when bombs were going off up and down the street, but now that things were calmer, roses (yes, roses!) in pots had appeared in front of some of the houses, and rays of sunlight were settling on windows framed with swirly organdy curtains.

Ahmed opened the door right away this time. "I need another suit," explained Ignacio. "When I get back home, I'll be wearing suits every day."

"Ah," said Ahmed. He took the tape measure from his teeth and put it down. "I already have the measurements."

"It needs to be resilvered," said Ignacio, pointing to the mirror. Actually, he said, "It needs to be repaired with silver on the back." He had learned the word in Arabic for "silver" and had practiced the sentence for several hours.

"Yes," said Ahmed, "but that's expensive."

Three days later Ahmed produced another beautiful suit, this one a blue merino number. Ignacio put it on and modeled it for the other lieutenants.

"Classy, Montez," said Ray Crenshaw, Ignacio's friend

since training at Twenty-Nine Palms.

"A little old-fashioned, don't you think? I mean, with those pleats in the front."

"I don't know nothing about fashion and neither does anyone else in Moosebridge, South Dakota, where I come from. But I sure wouldn't mind having a suit like that for weddings and stuff."

Ignacio hung the blue suit on the hook with the gray one and waited.

"You're wasting your time," said Crenshaw. "The guy'll take your money, but he still hates Americans."

The sheiks said the same thing. Ignacio went to community meetings to discuss ways in which the local people and the Marines could work together, but Ahmed never showed up. The sheiks who visited the tailor couldn't get him to change his mind. Who knew if he wasn't in cahoots with Al-Qaeda? they said.

Before long, Ignacio was once again trudging up the street to Ahmed's shop, this time with Crenshaw.

"*As-salam alaykom*," said Ignacio, when Ahmed opened the door. "I need a lightweight suit for when I get back. My friend, Lieutenant Crenshaw, wants one, too."

For the first time, Ahmed smiled. "Please sit down and look through the pattern books," he said to Ignacio cordially.

"That's quite a lot of money for suits," I said to my son.

"I thought it was a good investment, Mom."

"Well, you need suits for job interviews, now that you're out of the military."

"I needed Ahmed to cooperate with us."

The tailor took Crenshaw's measurements.

"Where are your boys?" asked Ignacio. "They're usually here with you."

"They went back to school. They've reopened the secular madrassas. All the children are in school, even the girls."

Ignacio was glad to hear it. He'd helped rebuild those schools destroyed by war.

"Tea?" asked Ahmed when he was done taking the order.

Instead of calling for Kayoosh, he led the men into the main part of the house, where cushions were arranged on a carpet. Ignacio and Crenshaw sat on the floor cross-legged. Before long, Kayoosh floated in like a specter, barefaced but eyes lowered. A plain white *dishdasha* covered her from neck to toe. On her head, she wore a black hijab.

"She was a beauty," remarked Ignacio. "High, sculpted cheekbones, skin the shade of light brown sugar."

Ahmed's traumatized old house was smashed and splintered on the outside, but inside hung tapestries of red, gold, green, and white, some a riot of flowers crowded against solid backgrounds, some an interweaving of arabesques and curlicues.

I imagine Kayoosh gliding across the room. I see her standing against the ornate walls, an elegant black-and-white onyx in a box of gaudy baubles. I imagine Ignacio straining to sip his tea and divert his gaze away from her face.

What can a mother do but imagine? When Ignacio went to Iraq for the second time, I knew little about the Awakening. I imagined him dodging bullets and bombs, as he had during his earlier deployment. I think that all mothers whose children are far away in exotic and dangerous places spend their lives imagining the worst. Now I imagine a different scene: Kayoosh cocooned in white, her smooth face framed in indigo. Kayoosh crouching by the Americans with a carved wooden tray upon which sit a teapot, three cups, and a plate of sweets Ignacio knows that Ahmed has been out of work for a long time. Sweets are a luxury. They are a sacrifice he has made for his guests.

Ignacio comments on the loveliness of the wall hangings. They have been in the family for generations, explains Ahmed. Ignacio is careful not to comment on the loveliness of the hostess or even to acknowledge her presence.

"Do you think," says Ahmed after a while, "that other Americans might want suits?"

"Maybe," says Ignacio. He must be careful not to give the impression he is bargaining: more work for cooperation with the Marines.

"Perhaps you have other friends who…"

"I will ask," says Ignacio quietly.

Within a week or so, a trickle of Marines, mostly enlisted men, began to make their way to Ahmed's tailor shop.

I imagine Kayoosh saying to her husband, "You know, in war bad things happen to everyone. It's not usually the fault of the men sent to do the fighting. Why don't you try working with the Americans? As soldiers go, they're not particularly cruel, and after all, they're bringing you business."

I don't know whether she actually said those things or not, but Ignacio told me that after that, every time he passed the tailor shop, he saw Ahmed busy at his sewing machine. Occasionally the tailor would look up and see Ignacio through the window. He would smile and wave, and often he would invite him in for tea.

About six weeks before he redeployed to the States, Ignacio began scouting around for a mirror.

"Where the hell are you going to find a thing like that?" laughed Crenshaw.

"I'll ask around the souk. Someone will know."

The carpenter Mustafa suggested they try his cousin Ali's antiques shop. The front of the shop had been badly damaged by a grenade, but miraculously, Ali had salvaged a few treasures he kept in a storage area in the back—among them, a large, oval mirror with a wooden frame decorated with interlocking triangles. It was fastened to a stand with hinges on either side that permitted the mirror to tilt. Two smaller side mirrors, each in the shape of a half oval, folded inward over the main glass, creating a large decorative panel. Ignacio haggled with Ali an hour or so. Then he and Crenshaw carried the purchase to Ahmed's shop.

Ahmed looked at the mirror a long time. His eyes had the pained look of a martyr at the rack.

"Come," he said finally. "I'll ask Kayoosh to bring tea."

The three men sat on the floor and sipped.

"It won't make me work with the Americans," said Ahmed after a while.

"It's a gift," said Ignacio softly. "I expect nothing in return."

"A nephew and two cousins," said Ahmed with a sigh. "The boy had a future. He would have gone to school, maybe become a lawyer, maybe a politician. And my cousins were like brothers to me."

"I understand."

"You can't understand."

"I want you to have the mirror, Ahmed. I've spent many enjoyable hours here with you. I wanted to give you a present, that's all."

"Thank you," Ahmed said softly. "It's a beautiful mirror, and very useful for my work."

Ignacio and Ray got up to leave. Ahmed embraced Ignacio, kissing him on both cheeks. "You're a good man," whispered Ahmed. "You helped me get my business going again. But war causes bad blood."

Ignacio squeezed Ahmed's hand. "Peace can make good blood," he whispered.

Then Ahmed embraced Crenshaw, and the Americans left.

The new unit of Marines was settling in, and Ignacio and his men were packing up. Days remained before they were to climb into trucks for the first leg of the journey home. From Baghdad, they would fly to Dublin and from there, to Charlotte, South Carolina.

Ignacio was addressing mailing labels when Crenshaw came running in.

"Hey, Ig! You'll never guess what I just saw!"

"An Iraqi woman in a bikini," muttered Ignacio dryly.

"I saw Ahmed walking toward the big Marine base, Hurricane Point! And you know what he was carrying? Swatches of fabric! Pattern books! His tailor's kit with measuring tapes and pins and stuff! He's going to sell his wares to the Marines!"

Ignacio chuckled. "He's a good person, Ray. You can't blame him for being bitter, but all Ahmed really wants is to work. Working is the only thing that will help him get through his grief. Anyhow, I hope he sees now that we gringos aren't such bad guys. And maybe eventually... eventually..."

I imagine Ahmed trudging up the dusty street, impeccably dressed in herringbone tweed despite the 108-degree morning sun. The tight weave of creases around his eyes slightly relaxed. His lips parted in an anticipatory smile. I see him explaining his business to the sentries, showing the gate pass secured for him by Lt. Ignacio Montez, shifting his sample swatches from one arm to another to show his ID, passing inside.

I imagine him back home, sipping tea in a room filled with ornate tapestries, orange, gold, green, and red, tightly packed with geometric designs and graceful Arabic writing. I imagine him embracing Ignacio, kissing his cheeks and murmuring, "You helped me get my business going again. *Assalamu Alaikom warahmatu Allahi wa barakatuhu.*"

"May God bless you as well."

* * *

It was a few months after Ignacio left the Marines that a package came, a rectangular box with a New Hampshire address. I called Ignacio at work.

"Who is it from?" he asked.

"The name in the corner is Rick Sabatini."

"Hmm, I don't know anyone by that name." I heard a barely perceptible tremor in his voice.

I began to worry. After Ignacio had returned from his first tour in Iraq, a package came with the shoes of a Marine killed in action. A young man named Ryan McCall, who had been a good friend of Ignacio's. Ryan had said that if anything happened to him, he wanted my son to have his shoes. I didn't really understand, and Ignacio never explained, but he kept the shoes in his closet, always dusted and perfectly shined.

When Ignacio got home, he looked at the package a long time, turning it over and staring at the address. Then he tore it open.

It was a suit. Perfectly tailored wool gabardine. The note read in Arabic: "For Lt. Ignacio Montez. From your friend, Ahmed."

Ahmed had given it to one of the men in the unit that replaced Ignacio's and asked him to send it to my son.

* * *

Now I look at the television screen, at the images of ISIS fighters garbed in black, knives in hand, and I remember that once there were two men from radically different worlds who sat on cushions and drank tea together. And I wonder where Ahmed is now.

Barbara Mujica

Barbara Mujica, professor emerita at Georgetown University, is a novelist, short story writer, and essayist. Her novel *Frida* (Overlook Press, 2001) was an international bestseller that appeared in eighteen languages and was a Book-of-the-Month Club alternate. Her novel *Sister Teresa* (Overlook Press, 2007) was adapted for the stage by Coco Blignaut of the Actors' Studio in Los Angeles. The play premiered in November 2013. Her novels, *I Am Venus* (Overlook 2013) and *Lola in Paradise* (in progress) were both prize-winners in the Maryland Writers Association National Fiction Competition. *I Am Venus* was a quarter-finalist in the 2020 ScreenCraft Cinematic Novel competition. Mujica has also won several prizes for her short stories, including the E. L. Doctorow International Fiction Competition, the Pangolin Prize, and the Theodore Christian Hoepfner Award for short fiction. Her story "Jason's Cap" won first prize in the 2015 Maryland Writers' Association national fiction competition. "Imagining Iraq" and "Ox" won prizes in previous years. Two of her stories were adapted for the stage by the Jewish Women's Theater in Los Angeles. At Georgetown, Mujica taught early modern Spanish literature. Her most recent scholarly books are *Religious Women and Epistolary Culture in the Discalced Carmelite Reform: The Disciples of Teresa de Avila* (Amsterdam University Press, 2020) and *Collateral Damage: Women Write about War* (University of Virginia Press, 2021). The mother of a Marine, Mujica was faculty adviser of the GU Student Veterans Association and co-chair of the Veterans Support Team. Her articles on veterans' issues have appeared in numerous publications. In 2015, she received a Presidential Medal from Georgetown University for her work on behalf of student veterans.

Breakfast Crisis
By David Parish

Neither of us spoke while driving to the diner, my mother quieted by stress, embarrassment and anger, all still in early bloom, and me mostly by nervousness. The atmosphere in the car was tense. We were both still sorting out our ruptured emotions, having staggered through the prior two weeks reshaping our identities around Larry's pronouncement that he was moving out and divorcing Marcia; news he dropped on mother in the kitchen minutes after she and I returned from early-summer, Saturday afternoon shopping. A heartbeat after delivering his divorce speech to me, he said he loved me, we shared a teary hug, he kissed the top of my head and was out the door. By the time I made it downstairs Marcia was on the phone with my grandparents. His parents, not hers, having decided that the best thing to do in that moment was to tell them, in a rattled voice, that Larry left us. I could hear wailing on the other side of the phone and figured that Grandma Pearl had not been in on the plan.

Our stretch of central Jersey was about a decade into its race from rural to suburban. Farm stands and pick-ups were making way for convenience stores, station wagons and elementary schools, as suburban neighborhoods popped up everywhere, pushing aside sod farms and apple orchards. Our house was one of those.

Did he call Shari, my older sister, to let her know what was going on, I wondered? I went back upstairs to wait for her to get home from her summer job at the mall.

Larry and I spoke on the kitchen-wall rotary dial phone every few days over those next two bizarre weeks, my mother hovering while we discussed nothing useful or meaningful or comforting. The conversations only added color to my confusion, like a paint-by-numbers project coming to life, but turning everything uglier instead of prettier while perfectly capturing a 70's era television drama vibe about a father and his estranged son. Him pretending to be chipper and curious about my summer days, buddy this and buddy that, while I squeezed out one-word answers, dying to hang up. Larry must have known that shameful details about the life he was actually living, as opposed to the pretend life we knew about, were becoming visible. Now, two weeks later, I was meeting him for breakfast. To talk. To clear the air. His idea.

Would we hug?

Would we pretend that meeting for breakfast was more normal than not and spend some time catching up on the

Mets, or would we go right after an elephant?

Something like, "Mom told me you moved in with a girlfriend. Your secretary." True. Apparently he forgot to make space for that chapter in the "I'm in a bad marriage - everyone deserves to be happy - I'm leaving - I love you" narrative, allowing it to be discovered hours or days later - I don't recall which - by my mother, who tossed it onto my rapidly growing pile of confounding life re-building blocks. That's not a criticism of her by the way. What's she going do? Hide it from me? Pretend I wouldn't find out from ... absolutely everyone?

I wish I could remember the moment more clearly as she came to a stop and I stepped out of the car in front of that diner. If Marcia said anything at all, it was probably ... distant. Emotionally flat. It's hard to believe otherwise, but I don't know. On her best days, my mother's emotional palette ranges tightly between determined and worried, so on this - pretty fucking far from her best day - a reassuring send-off seemed unlikely. It didn't matter. I wasn't listening. I was focused on trying to calm my nerves and was determined to not cry. Don't cry. Not in front of Larry.

It's absolutely true that I never, as in never-ever, had to make a single important life-shaping decision up until that morning; including the day Larry left. I was no more than a recipient of information about a change in domestic status, tossed at me like a newspaper flips onto your driveway. Like every suburban sixteen-year-old, at least the ones I knew, everything in my world was pretend-important but would not, ultimately, change much going forward. Not unless you did something like crash your car. Spoiled and sheltered were definitely top ten descriptors of me. But walking into that diner, I was stepping *into the game,* and the person who sat at the very center of my universe up until a few weeks prior, my father, was unknown to me. I knew that whatever was going to happen next was important in a way that was going to leave a mark.

My father. Those words stopped me for a moment, as if I scanned across an unrecognized phrase while reading in a half-learned foreign language. Even now, writing *my father* feels like a lie. Or a betrayal to ... fathers. The only *my father* I'm familiar with is wrapped in a ragged and slightly menacing, corrosive forty-year old memory. Writing those words somehow, for me, conveys some greater connection to the ideal archetype, making the concept seem more immediate or relevant or true. None of that really works in my world.

Maybe it's my inability to conjure an authentic positive emotional connection to the notion of *my father.* Discomfort penetrates the calm, triggered by a disconnect between the reptilian priorities that attach themselves to that phrase, assembled from traits like strength, protection, loyalty and love, and the vacancy of any similar emotional relevance to me or *for* me. There's simply nothing there, yet I know there's supposed to be, so it takes a moment to adjust. It's like imagining how it would feel to be 6'5" instead of 5'10". I can see it in my mind's eye – briefly, sort of – but dismiss it effortlessly as fantasy. Oh yeah. My father. I know what that's supposed to mean.

Larry, a bearish jowly man with dark thinning hair, was sitting alone at a table for two in the middle of the mostly filled diner, spinning his spoon in his coffee, wondering, I guess, how to reset a dashed relationship with his son. Did he feel a pang of anything when I pushed through the door? Had he glanced up to see Marcia driving away? How confident was he in that moment that what was about to happen would go well?

Anyone paying even a little bit of attention knew that Marcia and Larry had a terrible, awful non-fixable marriage. Truly, it was no tragedy that he walked out. That part came later. The dysfunction in their relationship was *visible* through their constant arguments but was *defined* by the undisguised disgust in their voices. Their rancor wasn't about having different values and goals. Each clearly resented nearly everything about the other. This was not the result of faded tenderness, or boredom or self-reflection with age. Their incompatibility grew from their souls and was about as changeable as gravity.

I have to imagine they married one another because there was a check list of requirements that kicked in at a certain age rather than softly lit halos of love dropped upon them by angels. No. This was about minimum acceptable requirements and a ticking clock. Nice looking, Jewish, suburban aspirations, lives nearby and wants a family. Check, check, check, check and check. But their differences were absolutely, scraping-the-bottom-of-the-lake fundamental.

Large, confident, loud and personable, Larry was forever trying to squeeze his authentic working-class presence into a white collar frame, but it never quite fit. He was everyone's street-smart pal who was a little simple but funny, a bit rough around the edges but just smart enough to be in on the jokes, mostly. If you weren't his perpetually disappointed wife, you probably thought of him as a good guy. There was also a leadership quality to Larry that showed up every now and then in unexpected ways; perhaps from the combination of his physical presence, likability and his willingness, anytime and anywhere, to speak up.

Marcia was more highbrow. Appearances mattered. She was born to immigrants, but there was nothing old-world about her and the upper middle-class expectations she carried. She was similar in some ways to her mother, Hilda, my grandmother, in their embrace of the rewards of a successful immigrant story. Hilda's sense of place, though, came naturally. Elegantly. She had earned it, and there was a comfort to how easily she melded old and new worlds, giving each their place. Marcia carried around the tension of believing she was, in some sense, a bit of an impostor. It was the difference between expressing high expectations of yourself versus feeling like you're entitled to something that's just out of reach.

It came down to this. Larry eventually saw that Marcia felt superior. He knew, and we all knew at some level, that she believed she was better, smarter and more deserving than him, his parents, his sister, her family and so on. That she had married down. And Marcia saw Larry as crude and a little dumb. Somebody who would never play it straight and was always trying to work the angles to get ahead. They were both right of course, but by the time they realized where they had arrived, it was too late. Two kids, a mortgage in the suburbs, college tuition around the corner and deeply invested in a sham aspirational family life that was about seventeen years in the making. Pressure building beneath the volcano's dome until it cracks open.

So, Larry left and I was sad because change and

uncertainty is hard, but it made sense. It actually seemed like the right move.

But then in no time at all, it didn't. It didn't make sense, didn't seem right, and Larry only vaguely resembled the person I spent sixteen years calling *my father* and meaning it. Instead, jagged pieces of reality crashed down on us repeatedly during those two summer weeks in 1977. Larry, we learned in bits and pieces from this friend or that, was the guy who left his family to move in with his secretary, who took a second mortgage on our house without his wife's knowledge and who borrowed money from everyone he knew, often telling them I - yes me, his teenage son - was having heath issues and the medical bills were overwhelming. He also feigned health problems of his own that would require a move to a drier climate, apparently to establish a cover-story with my mother for ditching town - still as a family unit, at that point - to avoid the shit storm, financial and otherwise, that he was assembling piece by piece. The blows to our world - to my world - were relentless in the days between the door closing on his way out and the door I pushed open while walking into the diner that morning.

He stood, we hugged, which embarrassed me, and I sat across from him. I have an image - real or not - of a waitress coming to the table.

"Do you want some orange juice, sweetie?", she asked with a smile in the stage show underway in my head.

She had to have seen the sideways energy spinning around that table. And not just from me; Larry was making his shit up as he went along. Did he ask his new girlfriend for advice before heading over that morning?

The juice arrived. We'd order food later. The waitress left, probably commenting to the others behind the counter about the uncomfortable vibe at one of her tables.

Silence. I sure was not going to speak first.

"I know you're confused and emotional and probably have a lot of anger right now. I wanted to see you so we could talk about what's happening and to make sure you know that even though your mother and I are getting a divorce, I love you and would never walk out on you. I'm still your father, and always will be."

Silence. Don't. Cry.

"You must have a lot of questions. You can ask me anything", he said, nodding. Smiling. "Go ahead."

Did he really say those words? I have no idea, but I'll tell you this. That's most definitely the general message he delivered over coffee and orange juice that morning while the diner buzzed around us. All credit to him. Larry said exactly what needed to be said.

I allowed an exhale. Ask away, right?

Well, there was really only one question that needed to be asked, and it didn't dance around the details of what happened or why or what any of us might expect next. I didn't care much about why he left Marcia - that they had a bad marriage was the one grain of truth in all of this - or the girlfriend or any of the other dreck. It didn't even focus on me. No. I went big picture. Though I didn't get it at the time, the question I had for Larry that morning was the Shakespearian dagger he never saw coming.

I went with Betrayal. Capital B.

"You lied. Big ugly lies. For years, about everything. To me and to everyone we know. That's what I don't understand. That's what I want you to explain. How does a father lie to his son like that? What am I supposed to take away from all of this?".

Those words, unplanned, were not the words of a suburban teen who had not yet become at ease in his own skin. No. They were the words of somebody who just completed a two-week, hands-on crash course in disappointment and hard knocks. They were the words of a pissed-off, full grown adult.

"I don't understand", I repeated. "Go ahead. Explain it to me."

The world shifted into slow motion as the weight of the moment, the heft of those words, crushed us both. Larry's face, his entire body, traveled from shock to anger and then fury. As his chair slid back across the linoleum floor and he rose from the table I was certain he was going to hit me. Or hoist me by my shirt to launch me across the room. I braced.

Larry stood 6'2" and was pushing two-thirty as he stood over me, furiously processing what I had just said. He remained still for a moment or an hour, struggling to dampen his anger, and then without looking away, clawed into his pocket for his wallet and threw some bills on the table before leaning down into my face, his eyes bulging, ears turning red and breath hot. His hatred in that moment could have supported a house. Though he was looking directly at me, there's no doubt that he saw my mother and everything he despised about her and their life together sitting at that table. That was the exact moment he flipped off the switch. I saw it happen. It was the instant he decided I was no longer his son and he was no longer *my father*.

"Who the hell", he hissed, loud and angry enough for everyone to hear, "do you think you are?" I recognized the disgust that sharpened the edge of each word out of his mouth. The loathing tone was exactly the same as when he and Marcia fought.

His question that wasn't really a question, more like a *fuck you*, hung alone in the dead-quiet diner for a moment and then he was out the door and gone. Again.

The restaurant had come to a full cinematic stop in those ten or twenty seconds. Everyone in the room had been tapped in the chest. I didn't notice any of them as I tried to convince my hands and legs to stop trembling. Trying to breathe. My mind went blank as my place in the world took a hard jolt and pieces of me were scattered about.

The waitress returned.

"Are you OK?", she asked, kneeling down so her face was near mine.

Don't. Fucking. Cry.

I nodded.

"Do you want to call somebody", she asked.

"My mom, I answered, my wavering voice almost unrecognizable. "I need her to come pick me up."

"OK. Come on", she said, leading me to the phone behind the counter, next to the cash register. "Use this one."

"Mom", I was saying a moment later, trying to sound in control. "You need to come get me. We're done."

I waited outside, trembles and chills skipping through my body while the emptiness where my stomach used to be continued to swell. "Did he hit you?" Marcia asked as I opened the door and slid into the front seat, not feeling the tears on my cheeks. She had been crying also. I shook my head.

"Are you alright?", she asked.

"I'm fine", I said, lying. Shutting down. To protect her?
To protect myself?

***

After more than forty years, I still sometimes wonder.
Am I alright? What would life have felt like had I not been
unknowingly searching for Larry's replacement ever since
that morning? Is he why I'm motivated mostly by fear of
failure? Is the abandonment I absorbed the reason I'm
convinced, at some level, that all good things that have
come my way will be yanked away? Abruptly. Harshly.

Probably, yes.

But then sometimes, I get to step away and see myself
in contrast to nearly everything that Larry represents. I get
glimpses of a version of me that's revealed though the love
of my wife and sons and our friends. Through my sister and
my mother. I even occasionally, not too often, have my own
moments of clarity, where I see how I refused to be his
victim and turned harsh lessons around. Not without scars
and questions. But still, into a life I would choose again
without thinking twice.

And then I realize that, yes. I'm just fine.

David Parish

Having transitioned over thirty years from psychology professor to tech entrepreneur to executive recruiter, David has pivoted once again to focus on writing short stories while tinkering with a novel. Other interests include reading (constantly), playing guitar (enthusiastically), meditating (aspiring) and learning Italian (passionately). He and his wife split time between home bases in Minneapolis, overlooking the Mississippi River, and Steamboat Springs, with a view of northern Colorado's stunning Yampa Valley. As time and pandemic restrictions allow, they would otherwise be traveling to visit their scattered children and to explore the world.

The Ping-Pong War
By Eric Rosenbaum

It's a little-known fact that I single-handedly turned the tide of the Cold War at the ping pong table of the Permanent Mission of the People's Democratic Republic of Outer Mongolia.

In September 1962, my family had moved from our suburban Long Island house to a skyscraping new apartment building on the Upper East Side of Manhattan. When the school bells rang for sixth grade, I walked through the doors of a dingy former public school building re-purposed to house the United Nations International School. Looking around me in the assembly hall, it was plain to see I had left the world as I knew it behind.

The school, established principally for the children of diplomats, was as advertised: a mini United Nations. The kids did not look at all like the kids where I'd come from. About the closest claim I had to membership in the international community was that the customers in my father's Lower East Side shoe store were mostly Chinese, Puerto Ricans, Orthodox Jews and West Indians. The only real diversity I'd been exposed to was Jackie Robinson's

Brooklyn Dodgers, the team I worshipped... until their unforgivable defection to Los Angeles.

I entered the classroom with serious misgivings about finding my place in this school where Americans were a minority, filling empty seats, contributing some local color, and paying full fare. My anxiety was immediately confirmed when I discovered the kid sitting next to me went by the name of Srinath Kizhkepat Wyjegenawardena.

Who was I going to be in this new world?

I decided to cast myself as a talented athlete.

I soon discovered the flaw in my plan. The only arena for establishing a reputation for athletic prowess in this school was at the ping pong tables. Every lunch period I'd take a few bites of the slimy baloney sandwiches or greasy "pizzas". Then I'd rush to join the crowd watching the competition of the elite members of the school's table tennis world.

Anyone who dared had the right to take their turn. As a sixth grade newbie in a school that went through twelfth grade, I wasn't about to opt for guaranteed humiliation; though I itched to play, instead of calling winners, I competed to become most valuable retriever of balls bouncing along unpredictable paths on the old, scratched up, rutted tiles.

My competitor for retriever-in-chief was my classmate,

Enkh (pronounced by us as "ink") J., son of the Ambassador to the United Nations from Outer Mongolia, who did not quite reach the modest height of my neck. After each point we scrambled to win the battle to retrieve the ball and quickly return it to the server.

"I got it!" I'd yell, shoving Enkh aside to run down one of the ferocious slams of Alesh from Hungary before the little ticking plastic ball slid through the open door leading to the girls' bathroom.

"I found it!" I'd call, exchanging elbow pokes to the ribs as we crawled beneath lunchroom tables to track down a shot spinning wildly off the padded paddle of Joji from Japan.

The superior speed I'd intended to show off on the basketball court or the baseball field carried me to victory. My on-target curveballs to the server gave some hint at what my athletic performance could have been in an American school. With me crowned as the ultimate retriever, Enkh had no choice but to retreat, claiming his place among the stars of the ping pong world... calling net balls.

One day not far into the school year, Enkh shocked us by calling winners, challenging Sumisakar, an agile ninth-grader from India. He must be crazy, we all thought. Doesn't he know what's in store for him?

Sumisakar, who had an annoying talent for ticking the stripes at the edges of the table, had Enkh lurching from one side of the table to the other, always about to return the ball, but never quite catching up to it. Predictably, he was skunked, his embarrassment brought to a speedy conclusion by the mercy rule shutout score of 7-0.

"That was good. You almost scored a point," I told him as we climbed up the Down stairway back up to our classroom.

He two stair-stepped ahead of me without a word.

The next day Enkh once again had the audacity to call winners, this time at the doubles table. He took up his position at the foot of the table, paddle in hand. No one came to join him. This was my chance… to be annihilated. "Go ahead, take your turn," someone said. No one moved. "Yeah, you. Take this." A paddle was thrust into my hand. Guaranteed humiliation.

We were on against the fearsome combo of Stuart, a crafty Englishman who dizzied the opposition by alternating shots from side to side and Elena, a Peruvian famous for her ability to coolly return the most ferocious of slams.

We stood motionless as their serves went flying by or we knocked into each other, blocking our partner's path to attempt a return of a scorched slam. By luck, or out of a minimum of pity, our opponents allowed Enkh to score a single point when one of his returns managed to barely clear the net and double digit dribbled, finally rolling off the end of the table. The witnesses to the massacre applauded We didn't say a word for fear of provoking worse punishment. Another mercy score crushing, 8-1.

I walked away from the table without looking up. It was obvious I should give up. Maybe in three or four years I could try again.

Enkh caught up with me on the staircase. He was grinning. "You and me. We're good partners." I laughed. We shook hands on it.

In the following days and weeks, we devoted ourselves to the game. Our objective was both modest and impossible, to become legends. All we needed to accomplish this lofty goal was to win one lunch period game of doubles before the year was over.

We would play an hour before the school bell rang, avoiding nosy observers; or in the privacy of the 38th floor of the UN Secretariat building; or in the musty basement of Enkh's home at the Permanent Mission of the People's Democratic Republic of Outer Mongolia; an elegant brownstone near Central Park, where our only spectator was a giant portrait of Sukhi Bator, the leader of Mongolian independence.

It wasn't long before our efforts began to pay off. Our days of mercy defeats were behind us; our opponents now had to score the regulation 11 points to beat us.

Mid-October came and with it the thirteen fear-filled days of the Cuban Missile Crisis. Every night the world watched the news on TV, deathly afraid of imminent immolation. Back in my suburban school, I practiced duck and cover nuclear attack drills, diving under my desk, crouching with hands over head as if that would provide protection from an all-obliterating mushroom cloud-producing blast. Now the fulfillment of that vision loomed. Was the mutually assured destruction of a nuclear war between the Soviet Union and The United States at hand?

For us Americans there was no question of "my country right or wrong". It didn't matter if we were only the plain vanilla seat fillers of the school with no fancy diplomat parents; weren't we the country that won the wars; the Land of Truth, Justice, Freedom? We knew our young, dynamic, invincible President Kennedy had to be right. And the stodgy, old, shoe-banging Soviet leader Khrushchev had to be wrong. We felt sorry for our schoolmates from the Eastern bloc. It was all too obvious. Communism is evil; they must be brainwashed.

As for the Iron Curtain kids, the nightly news broadcasts of attacks on civil rights demonstrators with bullwhips, billy clubs, high-powered fire hoses and vicious dogs sufficed, for them, as indictment of the system of government of the host country.

On both sides of the ideological divide, we kept our opinions to ourselves, however. We all understood the obligation to subscribe to the school's aspirational philosophy of "a new world in birth" where international harmony reigned. Talking openly about our opposing views would be playing with fire.

The crisis came to a head when the US Ambassador to the United Nations, Adlai Stevenson, issued his dramatic challenge to the Soviet Ambassador, "I am prepared to wait for your answer until hell freezes over", for the admission that nuclear armed missiles capable of striking the US mainland were on their way to Cuba, 90 miles from our shores.

The afternoon of that showdown at the UN, Enkh issued his own challenge down in the basement of his Mission home. We would play a best of three series of games.

"This is war," he said. "I play for Communism. You play for Capitalism. If I win, Communism will rule the world."

"And if I win?" I asked.

"Impossible. Capitalism will never win."

I wasn't entirely sure I was prepared to be the standard

bearer for Capitalism. But I was not about to become a traitor, either.

"OK. You asked for war? War is what you'll get! Communism will never win!"

Our ping-pong table confrontation of Enkh's red East paddle versus my blue West paddle was a nasty, sweaty battle. Each point was accompanied by a comment:

"That's the last time you'll get me with that one, Communist!"

"Try that again and I'll stick it down your throat, Capitalist!"

"Alright for you, Communist!"

"That was just luck, Capitalist!"

Every statement was punctuated by a choice curse word in Korean, learned from the master curser, our towering, prematurely pubescent classmate, Young Il-Lee.

At the end of two games we were tied at one game apiece. Then we traded point for point through the third, decisive game.

Tied at 21 all, with a two-point advantage needed to win, I lay the ball down on the table, covering it with my blue paddle. "OK, how about calling it a tie?"

"We will fight this war to the finish, Capitalist," he replied.

But it seemed we would never finish. On and on we

traded advantages, see-sawing on the impossible balance of deuce.

Needing one more point to press my advantage into victory, I exchanged a seemingly endless series of shots with Enkh; his impudent offensive moves always countered by my nick-of-time defensive responses.

Beaten into a corner, I caught sight of a wicked spinning slam slicing off Enkh's sponged red racquet toward the opposite corner.

I lunged across, whacking desperately as the ball ticked the white-striped edge of the table and flew off the corner.

I whirled around just in time to see the ball I'd hit spring off Enkh's side of the table, bounce over his head, and smack the portrait of Sukhi Bator right between his serenely wise eyes.

I was stunned. Enkh was stunned.

We stared at each other, neither of us knowing what to say. We looked down at the floor and around the room; tapped our feet; scratched our necks; twiddled our thumbs; frowned; sighed.

Enkh swallowed hard and cleared his throat. Without a word, he climbed up the stairs and out of sight.

I retrieved the ball and put it to rest beneath my paddle. Several minutes passed. Sukhi Bator stared down at me. Had the loss been too great a blow to Enkh's fierce

Mongol pride? Maybe I should make a discreet exit in the interest of international harmony.

At length, I heard footsteps descending the stairs. Enkh appeared, a plain manila envelope in his hand. "Take this," he said.

"That's okay," I said. "I don't..."

"It's yours. Take it."

When I didn't reach for it, he slapped the envelope into my hand.

I opened it.

One of the features of our school was that you could learn just about any language you wanted to. At that time, I had started learning Russian, so I was able to read the name written in Cyrillic script upon the color picture postcard of a man in military dress.

Гагарин.

Yuri Gagarin, cosmonaut. First human in space.

Next, there was a black and white photo on a postcard with another military figure. The handwriting was illegible, but it matched exactly the printed version of the signature running across the photo. Turning the card over, I read the name.

Титов.

Gherman Titov. Second human in space.

The only treasure I owned was a 1956 Brooklyn

Dodger yearbook. This was....

I was speechless. The spunky grin returned to Enkh's face. "You will remember your pal Enkh, huh?"

***

We never achieved our ambitious goal of establishing ourselves as table tennis legends. Soon after this ping-pong battle royale, Enkh J. the elder was called back home to Mongolia. My friend Enkh sent me one postcard, and I sent one back to him. Inevitably, we lost contact.

Many years later, a woman paying for a pair of shoes in the store I had inherited from my father showed me her tax-exempt document from the Mongolian Mission to the United Nations. I asked her if she knew Enkh J.

"Enkh J. is our country's Ambassador to the United Nations," she told me.

"Is that little Enkh J., or his father?"

"Little Enkh J.?" the woman asked.

"Never mind. Tell him to come see me. Tell him I need a partner to play ping-pong. He will understand."

The very next weekend, a hulking mustachioed man straight out of one of those movies with Genghis Khan and the Mongol horde walked into my store, wife and three children in tow.

I didn't expect him to recognize me. Sparing him from sorting me out from among the look-alike American shoe salesmen on the selling floor, I excused myself to my customer, dropped my shoehorn, and intercepted him.

While I squatted on my bench, assisting his wife as she tried on an assortment of shoes and boots, Enkh and I talked. He introduced his perfectly behaved children, and I bragged about my not so perfectly behaved ones. He asked if I'd kept up with any of our old schoolmates, and I couldn't recall with any certainty who among those who had been at the school in his day I was still in touch with -- aside from Srinath Kizhkepat Wyjegenawardena (a/k/a Sweepee). He told me about his previous ambassadorial postings in Moscow, Kinshasa and Lisbon, and by my lack of response, I confessed I hadn't been pretty much anywhere.

While the cashier was ringing up the sale of a pair of stylish high-heeled boots his wife had selected, I asked Enkh if he remembered that afternoon down in the basement of the building that was once again his residence.

He nodded.

"Did you ever wonder what I would have done if you had won?" I asked.

"Not really."

It had been such a long time ago. It was all too plain, we were really just strangers from opposite points of the world, with minimal parallel experience. For him, the school had just been a stop along the way. For me, it was the promised new world, the only world where I ever belonged. The American society I'd returned to had no mercy rules to mitigate the brutality of the assassinations of MLK and RFK; of My Lai, Kent State and Jackson State; of Woodstock turned to Altamont. It had been a hard lesson to discover the world I'd come to know was stillborn within the walls of my school.

I was about to tell him he had my ping pong triumph to thank for the conversion of the "People's Democratic Republic" to the post-Cold War "Republic" of Mongolia. But we were no longer on a footing for the teasing of childhood friends.

We shook hands and promised to keep in touch. But I knew we wouldn't. I felt a sadness. It was not just nostalgia for old times lost. It was a deeper regret.

In winning that ping-pong game, I had received those autographs, still my most valuable possessions. Every time I take them out of their plain manila envelope, I am reminded of Enkh's generosity of spirit in defeat.

As much as I cherish his gift, I can't help wondering what would have happened had little Enkh J. become the owner of my one and only treasure.

I picture him back home in Ulan Bator sitting on the floor with his school chums. They're snacking on goat milk and cookies.

He takes the 1956 Brooklyn Dodger yearbook out of the manila envelope. They don't understand a thing about baseball, but they're looking at the pictures of the 1955 World Championship victory of "the people's cherce, dem Bums", the first American team to break the color bar.

The perennial underdog Dodgers have overcome the quintessential capitalist, winning-is-everything New York Yankees. Dodger teammates, black and white, are jumping into each other's arms, hugging each other, pouring champagne over each other's heads, planting kisses on each other's cheeks.

It's the promise of a new world in birth.

I can imagine Enkh telling his pals it was his American friend who gave this to him. And it isn't true what they say about these capitalists. This American friend of his did not hesitate to give away his most valuable possession.

THE END

Eric Rosenbaum

Eric Rosenbaum has taught writing, adult literacy and English as a Second Language and Citizenship served as a program manager at several campuses of the City University of New York, at the New York Public Library, the 1199SEIU Health Care Workers Union and elsewhere. He received an MFA in Creative Writing (Fiction) from Brooklyn College. He has published flash fiction in several internet magazines. and in a feminist textbook for English language learners. He speaks three languages and has forgotten another three. He lives in Yonkers, New York with his wife, Manuela, with whom he speaks fluent Spanglish.

After working in 108 different jobs, he has recently retired. He is now besieged by the cries of legions of impatient stories waiting in his computer to be finished and brought out into the light of day. Otherwise, he spends his time communicating with fellow writers via Zoom, playing minor key harmonicas, laundering, and hanging out with his 2 year-old granddaughter.

You can follow his daily brief postings of observations and questions on Instagram: @mincedwords1.

My father said "Home is only partly place. It's mostly memories. You'll always have those..." They are and will forever be of ragged end-days of winter and the steamy breaths of horses in the cold barn; the atmospheric clashes of summer that silenced the calls of cicadas in the stand of oaks behind the house; fall's golden sunsets and circling red-tail hawks looking for one last meal before night fell ....and the early morning mists in spring that rose from the pasture like ..

Smoke from Indian Fires
By David Tarpenning

When I was five, we moved from in-town to a rural plot of land that stretched from our house on a hill, west to the muddy banks of the Arkansas River; from our back porch north to a stand of oaks --to a neighboring farm on the east. On the south, our front yard sloped toward one of the rutted dirt roads that stitched the county together.

This was Osage County, Oklahoma. *The Osage.* It was home.

Our small farm was bought with the few dollars my father had saved from his office job in the oil refinery across the river and by my mother's thrift. What we ate came from the garden, the orchard, the chickens and our one cow. What we wore came from her skill on the Singer treadle sewing machine. And the belief that held us together, even in despair, came from my parents' Baptist upbringing.

It was a time of broken promises and shattered dreams in America. The Depression was receding into history and there were no illusions about the future. Whatever it might be, we knew it would only be accomplished by endless work and grim resilience--for we had discovered long ago that there was no redemption in suffering, no sanctity in tribulation.

Men in *The Osage* worked hard jobs in the oil patch or in the refinery ---when they were lucky enough to find work. Their wives cooked on wood stoves and did laundry by hand with lye soap in tin tubs. Watching the clotheslines, neighbors kept up with one another--a row of khaki shirts meant someone found work. White shirts signaled that they were still looking. A line of aprons said someone was preserving what little was left in the garden.

What we did in *The Osage,* we did together. From flying homemade kites on the March wind to box suppers and barn dances in someone's hay loft in winter to the lap-and-tap horse races on a sandy county road in summer. We did it with joy, with thanks that we were living life as we saw fit. We took thoughtful care of each other, sharing what little we had. Our unspoken vow was that together we would fight to keep the best and defeat the worst, because what we had was worth preserving at any cost. We dared *anything* to take it from us.

And *anything* took the dare.

The beginning of the end came --virtually unnoticed--in an article in the *Daily News,* a Tuesday through Sunday newspaper published in the neighboring town of Ponca City.

"British RAF airmen are being assigned to U.S. airfields for flight training. With all airbases in Britain pressed into service by the RAF to fight the Germans, finding time to train new pilots is impossible. Ponca City is one of seven U.S. airfields chosen to provide the training because Oklahoma has over 320 days of flying weather each year. The more time the RAF airmen have in the air, the more success they will have beating the dreaded Luftwaffe when they return home."

Photos showed uniformed young Brits and the airplanes they would fly-- yellow PT-17 bi-wing Stearmans with greasy engines in front-- RAF painted on the underside of the bottom wing--- smiling, ruddy-faced, sandy-haired young men standing in front of their machines on the paved runway of the Ponca City airfield.

There was a back-story to the article--something we would not have understood, perhaps not even believed. Thousands of miles from America, across the Atlantic,

Britain was fighting a powerful and belligerent Germany. English cities and the once-peaceful countryside were pounded by the Nazis. Incendiary bombs, strategically targeted to industrial sites, were instead dropped indiscriminately--- burning cities and killing civilians. The Germans were destroying a nation. Winston Churchill became a familiar sight in our movie newsreels and on American radio. Squarely, he addressed the terrible suffering of his people, the loss of family members, friends...and their homes; at the same time rallying the Brits to resist and fight.

Far from our shores, it was someone else's war, not ours. The U.S. remained neutral despite Churchill's repeated entreaties. All across the country, Americans lived our lives, oblivious to a world determined to tear itself apart. In cities and towns, on the farms, in the factories, our young men were safe.

We took in the affable British airmen, inviting them to dinner, to church, to school events. We did our best to make them feel at home, but their yearning was long and deep, made worse by the trials of separation and fear for their families' safety in a shredded England. Maybe it was best that their rigorous flight schedules kept them busy during daylight hours and classroom instruction far into the night.

They trained daily, Monday through Saturday. Flying in

fours, their usual flight path took them over *The Osage*. They came up from behind our barn so low you could see the men inside, smiling and waving. They flew over our pasture, over the road south before turning north over the farm on the east. The children from across the road and I made a game of "chasing" the planes until we were out of breath and the roaring machines were out of sight.

In early fall, on the last carefree day before the start of school, we lined up at the north end of our place. At the first sound of airplane engines, we ran south laughing and waving at the young pilots. They dipped their wings in one last salute to retreating summer before flying east. As they turned back north, the engine of the fourth plane began to smoke. At first white puffs, then grey and finally thick black smoke streamed ominously from it.

The engine sputtered and caught, then sputtered and was silent. Spiraling toward the ground, the plane whined and shrieked, its superstructure stressed by excessive speed and an angle it was not built to accommodate. Briefly, it fluttered like a dying yellow moth before beginning a corkscrew to the ground at the edge of Clark's farm. It disappeared into the oaks and for one moment of fearful silence, there was hope. But flames erupted within the trembling trees. Two young men--the American instructor and his British student--were sacrificed to war's insatiable appetite.

Two days later, we gathered for a memorial service in the auditorium of the Ponca City civic building--men in suits or overalls, women in hats and gloves or feed sack dresses, nuns from St. Joseph's, severe in their black habits and white wimples. The British trainees and their American instructors, pale, somber, stoically hiding their grief. Children--unaccustomed to tragedy, trying hard to understand the *"why?"*

The service was solemn and moving. The First Christian Church choir sang *Eternal Father Strong to Save*. The pastor of the Abyssinian Baptist Church read the 23rd Psalm and the First Baptist minister gave the eulogy. We were dismissed by the priest from St. Joseph's. *"We beseech Thee to remember us in our sorrow, watch over and guide us in our daily efforts and bring us closer to Thee so that we may abide in Thy strength. Amen."*

With that simple supplication, we stumbled silently into the sunshine of an early fall afternoon, aware that we were not the same as we had been less than an hour ago-- aware that we were now living closer to war's brutality. How long could America stay out of the conflict--a month, a year?

The answer came far too soon.

Sunday, December 7th, 1941 seemed at first like every

other Sunday in *The Osage.* Mother sewed in a chair by the
window to catch the afternoon light. My father finished
reading the Sunday paper, saving the "funnies" for me. With
his permission, I turned on our old Motorola radio. We
could only get one station which meant there were two
choices: listen or don't. The Sunday afternoon program
was a concert by the New York Philharmonic Orchestra. *"If
you listen to it",* my mother promised, *"you may listen to
Edgar Bergen and Charlie McCarthy when it's over."*

About 3 o'clock, the music stopped abruptly and a
voice, shrouded in static, crackled across the airwaves.

*"We interrupt this program to bring you a special news
bulletin. The Japanese have attacked Pearl Harbor, Hawaii by
air, President Roosevelt just announced. The attack was
made on all naval and military establishments on the island
of Oahu."*

My father listened wordlessly, his face a grim mask I
had never seen before. It told me that what lay ahead would
be devastating. My mother sat quietly, sewing materials in
her lap, tears in her eyes.

The next day, President Roosevelt addressed the nation
over the radio.

*"Yesterday, December 7th, a date which will live in
infamy, the United States of America was suddenly and
deliberately attacked by naval and air forces of the Empire of*

Japan."

The U.S. was at war.

So began days of chaos as each American tried to process the new reality. There were no reassuring words. There was no *"It's going to be alright."* There was no precedent to follow. We would have to make it up as we went.

That winter, the nation began hemorrhaging young men. In movie theaters, the *RKO Pathe News'* images were of soldiers on stretchers carried through the smoke and flames of battlefield hell. Limp arms hung over the side-- swinging with the uneven movement of stretcher-bearers traveling ground roughly plowed by artillery shells and bombs.

Johnny Clark, only eighteen, from the farm across the road was the first of the young men in *The Osage* to go to war. And within a few weeks, a Gold Star Mother's flag hung in the Clark's window. Johnny would not be coming home.

The military draft was not conscripting married men, but my father was assigned an *"essential military occupation"* by the War Department. He was ordered to travel the western United States in search of oil, encouraging small refineries to increase their output and establishing supply routes to get oil to the coasts for shipping. But he would do it from Kansas in the center of the United States. We would have to give up the life we had created in *The Osage*, the life we loved---rip it up and move away.   There were tears and anger. There were questions. *Why?* But there were no answers. *That's just the way it is,* my father said, sadly. *There's nothing to be done about it.*

Within days, our big barn was empty, filled only with phantom sounds and the lonesome whispers of wind through the crack in the barn doors. The horses had been sold, loaded up and taken away. Gone was the laughter, the horses' quiet nickering, the impatient stamping of hooves eager to get on the road.

All that remained was a house empty except for large mounds of cardboard boxes. Movers came the next day and our life in *The Osage* was packed unceremoniously into a large truck and sent off to Kansas.

As we drove away into an unknown and unfriendly world, I took one last look out the back window of the car. *"Why,"* I asked my father bitterly, *"did we have to give up so much for this war?"*

He was quiet for a moment before he answered. *"Son, Johnny's sacrifice was much more than ours. He gave up his life."* And then, with a sad smile: *"After all, home is only partly place. It's mostly memories. And you will always have those."*

Prologue

Very early one spring morning in 2001, I was on a business trip to a small town in northeastern Oklahoma. Too late, I discovered I had missed my exit. The only thing to do was take the next road east and hope I could get back on track.

Glancing out the car window, I noticed that the area I was driving through looked strangely familiar. But then a lot of Oklahoma looks a lot like the rest of Oklahoma.

Just beyond a low rise, I saw it---a small house by the side of the highway, two front windows boarded up, one on either side of the door. A porch pillar had rotted away causing the roof to sag. With one "eyebrow" lower than the other, the little house had a quizzical look that asked, "*Will I ever be a home again?*" The big tin barn had doubtlessly long since rusted away; the oaks in back were overgrown. The years had taken their toll.

It was not just another abandoned rural ruin. I knew what it was because I knew what it had been: my childhood home in *The Osage.*

I pulled my car to the side of the highway and sat quietly, taking it all in. The sudden weight of remembering hit me with such force that I could hardly breathe. Though decades had passed, I had forgotten none of it, from the joyful moment we first saw the place until I watched

through a filter of tears as we drove away and the little
house became a dot on the horizon. All the years between
then and now became second-hand to memories of the life
we tried so hard to preserve in *The Osage.*

I took one last look before moving on because I had
work to do. In the hollows of the pasture, just as it had so
many years ago, the early morning haze hovered over the
land like smoke from age-old Indian fires, dissolving into
wisps that danced through the scrub cedars. Everything
had changed--yet in my mind, nothing had changed and I
could hear my father say *"Home is only partly place. It's
mostly memories. And you will always have those."*

###

David Tarpenning

With a Journalism degree from the University of Oklahoma in his coat pocket, David Tarpenning stepped off a bus at 3 a.m. August 18, 1956 into adulthood at the U.S. Naval Officer's Candidate School in Newport, R.I. Six years later, his service as a Navy Public Information Officer over, he entered the real world as an advertising practitioner. Soon there was a family (two beautiful daughters and now seven incredible grandchildren!) With only his journalism degree and bravado, he opened his own advertising agency and for two decades, it was a satisfying career.

When he was asked to teach advertising full time at OU, it presented an opportunity to make a difference in charting the career path of bright, eager students. Twenty-one years and almost 10,000 graduates later, he retired--with the opportunity to exercise his passion for writing. He has now been published in the 2019 *Stories Through the Ages* anthology, *Chronicles of the West, Catholic Digest, Columbia Student Press Review, Computer Bytes, American Educational Journal...*and a 2018 Honorable Mention for his novella, *What Have We Become,* in *Glimmer Train's* fiction contest.

Contact info: *dtarpenning@gmail.com, ddtarpenning.com*

The Illustrated Man
By Jim Tritten

It had been a hard day. I downed one of those pills that would make me relax. Well, maybe two—what a day. The chairs in the Phoenix film studio had been uncomfortable. Thank goodness it's only a short evening flight to Albuquerque. I walk through the cabin closing in on seat 24B. Should be ahead on the right—an aisle seat. I can finally stretch my legs—easy access to the lavatory. Perhaps someone interesting. Someone to help me take my mind off the terrorist movie plot. Maybe that rather unusual-looking....

The first thing I noticed was his sweaty bald head as he mopped it with a white paper napkin. He looked up, and we made eye contact. I smiled politely. In return, his wide grin revealed a gold front tooth. He turned back to his submarine sandwich, stuffing the remainder into his mouth, while crumbs and condiments rained down on his lap.

I swung into 24B, adjacent to his window position. The smell of grilled onions welcomed me. I glanced to my left. Grease drooled from his lips, down his chin, and onto his black T-shirt. *Just my luck, there's no seat between us.* The white napkin returned to his pate, and he again wiped sweat. Perspiration saturated the paper.

I craned my neck searching for an empty place. *Perhaps there's a couple who wants to sit together. I'd trade places. No, that won't work; only two seats on this side of the plane. Maybe there's a couple who doesn't want to sit together.*

The flight attendant confirmed my fears. "This flight is completely full. Please place your carry-on luggage in the bin overhead or under the seat in front of you."

When she said a full flight, does that include first class? I've got enough miles for an upgrade.

"The captain has closed the door. Please fasten your seat belts and turn off all electronic devices."

I pretended to look past my neighbor out the window at the ground crew as the plane rolled backward. He was probably in his early thirties—no facial hair like I have.

Oh! Tattoos. How did I miss these?

They ran up from under his T-shirt onto his neck, reaching up to the base of his skull—reminded me of wisteria climbing a giant oak. More crept down from his short sleeves, practically obliterating any unmarked skin. Mostly blue ink with a smattering of red intertwining the designs and words. His powerful, greasy fingers sported a variety of polished steel rings. One featured a skull and crossbones.

"Good evening, this is your captain. The flight to Albuquerque will take forty-five minutes. We expect clear skies and no turbulence."

Really? Not from where I sit. I reached up and turned on the air conditioning, shifting the flow to the left ever so slightly. I tightened my seatbelt and clenched my jaw.

"Whatasuv he saoidnag hwu lungae to Alvaquanaiue?"

My travel companion creased his brow, suggesting that whatever he said was a question. *What did he say?* The man was mumbling. I looked to my left, and again we made eye contact. Grease continued to drip down from his lips.

"Whatasuv he saoidnag hwu lungae to Alvaquanaiue?" he repeated while airborne saliva, caramelized onions, and meat flecks flew at me. Probably a Philly cheesesteak.

This time I caught a glimpse of studs in his tongue as he attempted to verbalize what I surmised were words in English. *What's he asking me?* I ventured a guess.

"I think the captain said we would be airborne for about forty-five minutes. With taxi time, we should be at the gate in an hour."

"Thasnilk" His head nodded up and down. He smiled, and the gold in his mouth shone. Then he coughed into the formerly white napkin depositing green chunks of what

were probably either chiles or jalapenos.

No wonder he couldn't speak straight. Too hot for you, heh?

The engines roared, and we rolled forward on the runway. Out of the corner of my eye, I saw the nasty napkin get scrunched up and put inside the greasy waxed paper from his sandwich. He stuffed the mess into the magazine pouch at his knees and wiped his hands on his shirt—first the palms. Then the backs and then each finger. His biceps and forearm muscles were well-developed. Each flexed animating his illustrated skin. *Wonder what they'll look like when he's seventy?*

I closed my eyes and stroked my beard and mustache as we lifted off into the moonlit skies.

After reaching cruising altitude and being alerted it was safe, I unbuckled my seatbelt and leaned forward to reach under the seat in front. My backpack containing my iPad was wedged firmly underneath. His leg bent into my space and blocked my backpack. As my head twisted to the left, the chrome studs of the man's leather trousers reflected the overhead reading lights. His trouser legs were tucked into high black leather boots. A slack, polished chain ran down the side of the pants, affixed by a bolt screwed into the heel of his boot.

"Excuse me, sir. Would you please move your leg so I can get my backpack?"

"Oh coirhsaj," he muttered as the offending limb retracted into his domain.

I reached down and pulled out the backpack. As I withdrew my iPad and put it on my lap, the man took out a large smartphone. He held it close to his face. *Wonder what he's looking at?* If I pushed my head back into my seat, I could detect he was playing some kind of game. It had his attention. His thumbs continued to press buttons, eliciting an occasional animalistic grunt or groan from the player. The red wallpaper on his phone had a black circle in the center. Inside this circle, there was a white design— blocked from view by the game. My eyes widened as I realized the tips of the design in four distinct corners were the edges of a swastika inside the black circle.

All thoughts of using my iPad were replaced by searching my memory for what I knew about the Aryan Brotherhood. The Brotherhood used swastika tattoos. *They grew out of prisons—have they moved into New Mexico? Which tatt is awarded after the initiate kills his first victim? What if I told him I used to own a Harley?*

Maybe he's a Hells Angel? Too bad I couldn't read the lettering on the T-shirt. I used to wear leather trousers when I owned a Harley. I never wore a helmet and often rode with a cop back in D.C. Hadn't thought about that cop for years. He had been shot while trying to arrest a killer.

The illustrated man is a paid killer. Yeah, that's it. A hitman hired by the patrónes, the Hispanic bosses, coming into Albuquerque to do a job. Probably drug-related. So how will he get a weapon to do the job? Did he check it with his luggage, or would he pick up a clean piece in New Mexico? Not like it's hard to get a weapon in our state. He would have some new type of weapon they write about in all those thrillers—a Glock. I think most of them use Glocks. Or an Uzi.

The flight attendant broke my thoughts. "Sir, would you like to have a beverage?"

"Yes, give me a rum and coke. No, make it two". *What I really need are more pills.*

"Ikansgpu anseu cocknue?" The man eyed my soft drink as it was handed to me.

The flight attendant looked puzzled and then smiled as she replied, "The attendant up front has the coffee. I'll get you some in a minute."

"No, Ikansgpu anseu cocknue?"

I sensed the illustrated man wanted a Coke like mine and suggested, "I think he'd like a Coke."

Good guess. I wouldn't want hot coffee if my tongue had been burned already by that sandwich. The illustrated man grunted, and I was rewarded again with another look at his gold tooth. The attendant served him a Diet Coke, and I kept my mouth shut when he accepted it without comment.

I mixed my drink and emptied the plastic cup. I leaned back and closed my eyes. *Okay, calm yourself.* The drink felt good as the cold liquid went down my throat and into my churning belly. The second tasted better, but not enough to quench my unsettled mind. Before I knew it, I was off to the races again—monkey brain bouncing ideas off the inside of my skull.

I knew we all went through the TSA security check. *He doesn't have a weapon on him right now. But why would the agents allow an obvious killer like this to get on the plane? Don't we have the right to sit in safety?*

Don't the counter agents have some kind of profile this guy should have met? Why did they give him a boarding pass? See if I ever fly this airline again.

Is there an air marshal on this plane? Yeah, he can deal with this guy. I don't have to. Not my job. I'm retired. God, is this plane hot.

The man clicked away at his game. *How many kills was he getting? Was he whacking them or shooting at them like in the old Atari Space Invaders? Maybe the game was a ruse, and what he's actually doing is planning a mass murder in Old Town. That's it; the white supremacists are going to make a statement about the takeover of America by Hispanics. No, wait, the Spanish were here first in New Mexico. Is this guy the mysterious highway assassin who was shooting drivers on the Phoenix interstates last week? I need to warn them.*

I unbuckled my seatbelt and was about to get up and talk to the cabin attendant, but I was interrupted.

"Wharoaiun asnuagub kounuean?"

Again his eyebrows rose. I guessed it was a question.

I put my finger in my ear, raised an eyebrow, and frowned.

"Wharoaiun asnuagub kounuean?"

Better not offend this killer. What does he want? I offered an answer. "We should be on the ground in about a half-hour." He grunted and went back to planning mass murder.

Or is he planning my murder? He probably knows a dozen ways to kill me in my seat. He could put a knife between my ribs and deflate one of my lungs. I saw a show on the television where the victim never even felt the blade. No, he can't have a knife on the plane. But if he takes one of his thick arms and reaches around my back, he could snap my spine. Stop it.

I leaned forward and felt behind me. The man looked at me. I put my iPad back into my backpack, then put the backpack under the seat in front of me.

So if this guy is, in fact, a hired killer, does he know that I know? Will he need to silence me before he gets off the plane? He will have to make it seem like an accident.

I moved as far over to the right in my seat as I could and closed my eyes. The drinks and the pills began to work, and I was enveloped in total silence, blackness, and the faint smell of caramelized onions.

The bump of the landing brought me back to consciousness as the plane touched down. I felt along the left side of my torso for any sticky wet spots—my fingertips were dry. *So far, so good. I pulled out my backpack. The plane taxied into the ramp area. Jesus, why is this taking so long?* After it stopped, I got out of my seat and stood patiently in the aisle–my eyes firmly fixed ahead.

The other passengers hurried from the plane. I rudely pushed ahead of anyone I could and bolted down the aisle to safety. The aircraft deck shook as the heavy boots behind me thudded in cadence with the light touch of my Birkenstocks. *Why didn't I wear closed shoes? Is he going to follow me outside to the parking lot?* I raced down the corridors of the terminal, aware of the internal pressure directing me to find the nearest toilet. *Is it safe?*

I lost the sound of boots as I whisked through the turnstile, passing close by the TSA agent monitoring the portal. *It should be safe now.* I stopped and turned around. Nothing. The illustrated man wasn't anywhere in sight. I let out a long sigh and wondered how the agent could have helped. *Don't they know there are people in mortal danger here? I ran into the bathroom.*

Stay in the bathroom until everyone claims their luggage and leaves the terminal. That was the plan. Might as well be safe than sorry.

After what seemed an eternity, I emerged from the bathroom. Directly in front of me, my eyes spied the familiar black T-shirt and leather trousers of the illustrated man walking toward the escalator. The polished chain swung loosely at the side of his leg. A glint of light reflected from his gold tooth. *He's still here.*

I slid into an alcove, steeling myself for defense should he turn and spot me. I peered around a potted plant. The man held hands with a beautiful, tall woman about his age. She was slim and wore flowers in her long wavy blonde hair, which flowed freely as she chattered. She wore a pale blue and white dress that danced to the rhythm of her step.

Alongside the woman, five young giggling children skipped, carrying toy bears in their arms. They bobbed for attention alongside the couple as they moved toward the escalator.

One of the little children pointed at me, grimaced, and cried. The tall blonde woman glanced at me, picked up the child, and as they continued forward, I heard her say, "He's probably a nice man. We shouldn't be so quick to judge."

I watched the tall woman, and the illustrated man disappear from view as they ascended the escalator.

Jim Tritten

Jim Tritten retired after a forty-four-year career with the Department of Defense, including duty as a carrier-based naval aviator. He holds advanced degrees from the University of Southern California and formerly served as a faculty member and National Security Affairs department chair at the Naval Postgraduate School. Dr. Tritten's publications have won him forty-three writing awards, including the Alfred Thayer Mahan Award from the Navy League of the U.S. He has published six books and over three hundred chapters, short stories, essays, articles, and government technical reports. Jim was a frequent speaker at many military, arms control, and international conferences and has seen his work translated into Russian, French, Spanish, and Portuguese

Living Springs Publishers

We hope you enjoyed this book. Please let us know what you think about it. You can leave a review on Goodreads, or wherever you purchased the book.

This is the fourth edition of our Baby Boomers Plus book. The number of submissions to **Stories Through The Ages Baby Boomers Plus** has increased dramatically over the four years we have conducted the contest. Each story is read by at least three judges. We receive stories from people just starting to write and from those who have won many awards. The competition is intense, and the judges agonize over their choice, realizing the heavy burden of being fair but decisive. There are winners and losers, that is the nature of a contest. We thank each and every author for the stories they submit and urge everyone to keep writing.

You can find information about our contests and buy our books at www.LivingSpringsPublishers.com.

Living Springs Publishers is a family owned, independent publishing company based in Centennial, Colorado. Our mission is to help authors, regardless of age or experience, share their gift of writing. Using our expertise in editing and publishing we help our clients bring their stories and manuscripts to life.

www.ingramcontent.com/pod-product-compliance
Lightning Source LLC
Chambersburg PA
CBHW071556110726
47908CB00007B/2126